When You Can't Trust HIS Heart

Discovering the
Limitless Love of God

To Marina,

MARCI JULIN

Marci Julin ☺

Jude 1:1-2

Cover by Caleb Julin and cover picture by Michael Ikegami

Learn more information at:
www.HeartandMindMinistries.com--Bible teaching for women by Marci Julin

Dedication

For Angie Mabe, the Christian counselor whose
insightful challenge for me *to choose to trust God's
Word when it spoke of His unconditional love* led to a
complete transformation in my relationship with my
Father and prompted the writing of this book.
Thank you.

Also for my husband, who like my Heavenly Father has
loved me whether I have deserved it or not, and
whether I have recognized it or not. *Many a man claims
to have unfailing love, but a faithful man who can find?"*
Proverbs 20:6 I have found such a man.
I am truly blessed.

Contents

> "He who is wise, let him consider the great love of the LORD." Psalm 107:43

Part 1: Struggle

Part 2: Power

Part 3: Love

Part 4: Trust

Acknowledgements

Many people came alongside me in the endeavor to bring this book to completion, and to all of them I am deeply grateful. First and foremost, my husband Seth--the one I consider the true and gifted writer, edited and gave tremendous input and assistance for the entire manuscript from its infancy to its completion. I would also like to thank Joanna Harris who took the time to edit a number of my chapters and from whom I learned a new perspective on the style of writing, which brought balance to my work. Cathy Robertson also took the time to give some editing feedback in the early stages. Thanks also to my much loved mother, Linda Kissel and mother-in-law, Connie Julin who both gave me encouragement from the beginning. Thanks also to Michael Ikegami who patiently worked at capturing the image for the cover of the book. And last but certainly not least, thanks to my talented & creative son Caleb who created the book cover for me.

Part 1

Struggle

CHAPTER 1

A Devastating Thought

Like a goldfish in a bowl, for years a thought kept circling in my head. Sometimes it paused to rest, only to resume its course later. Imagine a fish's response to the addition of an aquarium ornament. The novelty of it would certainly draw him for a time, but then he would be back to the same relentless path. Similarly, positive changes in my life briefly interrupted the familiar thought patterns, but never for long. I am not sure when this thought was first born, but over the years it grew, fed by the continued difficulties of life.

In its early stages, the thought was, more than anything, just a simple realization: Life is hard. Gradually, that three-word thought grew more complex and infinitely more personal to become: *I, Marci Julin, seem to be God's chosen target to which He has cruelly hurled every dart and arrow in His arsenal.* Paranoia? Perhaps. But this thinking was not without basis. Difficult times convinced me that God had it out for me. In time I discovered that many others have similar fish swimming around their bowl.

Maybe you have had similar thoughts as a result of hard times in your own life. Whether it is the loss of a loved one or a lengthy illness, abuse endured or a failed marriage, loneliness or a rebellious child, consuming guilt over past sins or the consequences those sins inevitably bring--suffering in any form leads to a variety of questions and emotions. The truth is that life is hard. Everyone's response to suffering proves unique. Still, the heart-wrenching struggle with God over the difficulty or seeming injustice of our pain remains the same from one individual to another.

Why Lord? What did I do to deserve this? Will it ever end, and will I survive until it does? Actually, maybe I don't want to live through this. Do you just hate me, God? Left unchecked, questions and thoughts like those can morph from tiny goldfish into ravenous sharks with razor teeth. Such thoughts can consume us and devastate our ability to walk closely with God. After all, who wants to walk next to someone they do not trust?

Trust Scenarios

Picture with me for a moment, two scenarios. In the first scene we see a woman leaving a store in the city. Intending to walk home, she moves down the sidewalk with her arms full of groceries. Glancing over her shoulder, she spots her neighbor, and her brow furrows with worry. If only her expensive high-heels could be magically replaced with a practical pair of flats that would allow for a quicker escape.

If I hurry, maybe he'll just give up, she anxiously thinks.

Hi, neighbor, his voice calls out to her from behind, ruining any hope that he has given up his pursuit.

In her distress, she squeezes her bag too tightly and out pops the loaf of rye bread previously balanced on top. Unfortunately, by the time she resituates her bags and picks up the loaf, he is beside her. As he offers to help, she accepts the inevitable: He will be walking her home.

She keeps her distance as much as the sidewalk will allow. Nervously, she mumbles the required responses to his attempts at dialogue. Head down and eyes darting back and forth, she endures the walk home. If he notices her distress, he does not show it. Although her neighbor appears to be a kind man, albeit a little odd, anxious thoughts consume her.

Now the scene changes. We see a father walking hand in hand with his four year old daughter. Her little hand is encased in her father's massive calloused one. At 6'4'' and 225 pounds, made hard from years of moving furniture for a living, he makes an imposing figure. The child, oblivious to any causes for concern, chatters endlessly about her day at pre-school. Smiling, her father listens, all the while scanning their path for any possible dangers.

The girl begins to skip along but abruptly comes to a stop when her pink back-pack bounces heavily.

Daddy, she chimes, *Will you carry this for me so I can skip?*

With the transfer complete, she places her small hand back in her father's and resumes her care-free skipping.

Three blocks later, her steps slow and her words grow fewer, replaced now by the occasional yawn. It has been a long, exciting day. Sensing her tiredness, her daddy tenderly scoops his little one into his arms where she contentedly nestles the rest of the walk home.

Now granted, I chose scenarios at the far ends of the *trust* spectrum, but which would more closely depict your walk with the Lord? Like the trusting child with her father, do you find your daily walk free of anxious thoughts, completely trusting in God's sovereign control over the events of your life? Is it possible that you're fine trusting God only as long as life is good? Or, maybe like the woman in the first scene, your walk with God is generally characterized by anxiety or even a determination to handle things on your own? Are you like I was, wishing to live without fear but rarely succeeding?

I once saw a movie that followed the events of a good woman's life from her teen years to old age. Generally speaking, the story mirrored the lives of many people. As a girl her life was fairly idyllic. Things changed though, when, as a young woman, she lost her first love. From that point on she endured one loss and heartbreak after another, well into her old age. It is not like her entire life was a disaster. In fact much of her adult life was spent as a happily married wife and mother. Sadly though, the blessings and joys through the years never quite balanced out the pain of multiple tragedies.

How could that be? Each new tragedy brought her increasingly into struggle with her Maker because the pain had a cumulative effect in her life. In her mind the second trial was not just an isolated incident that brought suffering, but it was compounded by the memories of the first hardship, and so on. Even in good times, it was as if she was holding her breath, waiting for something to go wrong.

My life story has not been so different from the movie character's, but the ending is vastly different thanks to the life-changing power of God and His Word. In this book, I openly share the depth of my pain in order to illustrate the power of the biblical truths that brought about tremendous healing.

My Story

As a seventeen year old, I went on a summer mission trip to India. My evangelistic team bicycled to outlying villages to share the Gospel. The people lived in one-room, round, mud and thatch huts and "entertained" the strange foreigners outside. In spite of their tremendous poverty, they hospitably gave us bananas and chai tea at every home we visited. That made for a lot of bananas!

After six weeks, and with two more to go, our team's porcelain water filter gave out from the endless scrubbing necessary to purify the water. Our leaders resorted to boiling and bleaching the water. It would not cool beyond lukewarm, and the bleach coated our tongues when we drank it. In one hundred plus degree heat and pervasive dust we short-sighted teens soon gave in to drinking the cool, unfiltered water. Of course, my team all became gravely ill with dysentery and two people even contracted hepatitis.

That summer began my downward spiral of ever-increasing pain and illness for the next nineteen years of my life. One symptom led to more symptoms until there was no sorting it all out. As my adult years progressed so did the number of diagnoses. Through the years, doctor after doctor tried one test and recommendation after another, all to no avail.

Because I am a person who thrives on activity and accomplishment, I kept going full-tilt anyway for most of those years, always pushing myself through the pain. During that time, usually only God and my family saw the hurt etched in my brow at the end of the day and heard my cries for relief. Many nights I woke myself up crying from the pain that never ended. Can you imagine nineteen years of living with daily pain, making all areas of life a struggle?

The ability to continually push myself came to a screeching halt in 2004 as a result of an injury that herniated a disc in my low back, pinching a nerve. Those who have experienced an injured disc can testify to the all-consuming nature of such pain. I also began having excruciating pain after eating, which landed me in the hospital for more than a week on two occasions. At that point, I was severely anemic, had failing adrenals, and was too weak to stand or walk without help.

Dealing with relentless pain is one thing, but being unable to feel useful or even to have fun with my family was agonizing. After all, I was young, a wife and mother, and supposed to have a lifetime ahead of me to anticipate. Instead, I dreaded the future and prayed that God would just take me.

For a solid year I sought relief from the pain of the herniated disc and pinched nerve by resting on ice or heat in a recliner by my bedroom window. Since I hardly had the strength to walk or stand, that chair became my haven. God had brought me to the end of being able to distract myself with activity. During this period of seclusion and incapacitation, I had plenty of time and motivation to fervently seek the Lord. Staring out the window, hour after hour, day after day, I pleaded with the Lord for answers. But let's be real: It seemed absurd to believe that God could love me when He allowed such agony in my life.

Trust me, I read my share of books on the problem of suffering, and found temporary enlightenment and encouragement. Such books taught me to view the struggles of this earth as momentary in light of eternity. Although I must say, once you get past ten years of constant pain, it does not feel so momentary! Another common theme of books on suffering was that God could use my situation to bring Himself glory. These and other helpful truths did shift my focus...for a time.

Inevitably, I continued to come back to the same old struggle: I did not feel truly loved by God. I had heard the saying, *When you can't see His hand, trust His heart.* That is true; I had no doubt, but what if I did not feel that I could trust His heart?

This problem I had with God was not based solely in my physical pain. The physical pain only compounded the inward pain of a separate issue, a specific traumatic time in my past. Eight years earlier, at the end of 1997, I had been falsely accused of child abuse by a vengeful doctor.

It all began several months before the accusation when my three year old son, Caleb, became ill. The energy that usually characterizes little boys began to fade in Caleb. He ran low grade fevers constantly, had difficulty walking, and complained endlessly of leg pain. Needless to say, we were concerned.

Visits to the pediatrician began. Initial test results were inconclusive, and the doctor recommended that he see a specialist. No problem, right? Wrong! We belonged to an HMO that would not approve a specialist and our finances were too tight to pay for it. Born out of a mother's fear for her child, my insistence that something be done ASAP caused the doctor to become unhelpful. We were at a stalemate.

With great care, my husband, Seth, composed a letter to the insurance company in hopes of convincing them to appeal the decision. Never dreaming of the ramifications, Seth briefly mentioned the difficulty we were having with the pediatrician. Apparently the HMO looked into it, which greatly angered the doctor.

In retaliation the pediatrician accused me of a rare psychological disorder called Munchausen Syndrome by Proxy. Supposedly, that mental illness causes someone to make their child ill to gain attention for themselves. Little did we know that a "witch hunt" was on in our metropolitan area due to two doctors in our county who had just published a book on this condition. In our county alone, over two hundred women had been before the judge for this same accusation. So much for a rare disorder!

All of those details were unknown to us until one day, early in December, 1997. While I did laundry and my little guy played happily on the floor, we heard the fateful knock on the door. Being social by nature, Caleb's face lit up in anticipation at the thought of someone visiting. To our shock, it was a state case worker with disturbing questions and news that led to months of agonizing circumstances for our small family. Ironically, by this point Caleb's health seemed to be improving.

At the advice of our attorney, Seth and I fled our home with our toddler to prevent the state's capture of him before we had a chance to prove our innocence. Our attorney explained that it was legal for human services to pick up our son without warning. It was also legal for us, because there was not yet a court order, to make him unavailable by being elsewhere when they came looking for him. We fled immediately. We left our home, just decorated for Christmas, and found shelter with family and friends in multiple states for the next several months.

One of the many painful episodes from that ordeal was subjecting ourselves, under unbelievable stress, to a three-day psychological evaluation. Like bugs under a microscope are studied to see how they behave when poked, we were all individually scrutinized for hours on end. It was exceedingly difficult to sanely describe what inkblots on a page made me think of while keeping at bay the fear that threatened to overwhelm me.

Three thousand dollars and three exhausting days later, we went into hiding again and anxiously awaited our hearing. For a week, we desperately attempted to build our case and prepare ourselves as we hid in a small lake cottage in town. We tried to be strong during the day to keep our son free of worry, but usually broke down and sobbed ourselves to sleep at night. We knew, according to the precedent of all two hundred other cases of Munchausen accusations, that we were almost certain to lose our precious child in a matter of days. Every conceivable option was considered to avoid that likely fate but eventually discarded after much counsel and prayer.

The long dreaded day arrived. Armed with the psychologist's good report and overwhelming testimony on our behalf, we arrived at the juvenile courthouse on a February morning. The hearing, scheduled to last a mere thirty minutes, continued off and on all day. By the end of the day our innocence was so apparent that even the bailiff and the state's case worker were in tears at the ruling. The judge, citing carefulness, determined that our one and only child should be placed in foster care. I wondered how a loving God could allow such a travesty to occur.

Later that night the foster parents had to physically restrain our three year old son who pleaded with wrenching sobs for us not to leave him. He was so small and helpless, and we were helpless to save him. Devastated, we had to leave knowing that he did not understand why he must be separated from all he knew and loved. Refusing to be comforted, my toddler sobbed alone that night, and many others as well, while his foster mother sat helplessly in the hallway listening and praying. Caleb would not even allow the kind foster mom to wipe his nose during those episodes. Through tears he yelled at her, "No! That's Mommy's job!"

While living in others' houses for three seemingly endless months, I longed to be in my own familiar home again. My longings, however, did not include the scenario that came to pass. That devastating February night my precious baby was across town, and my husband and I went home to an empty house. The next morning, Seth dragged himself back to work, and I faced a day alone. As I looked at the long dead Christmas tree and neglected decorations, I knew this day marked the end of my desire or willingness to cling to God and His Word.

I had clung to God's comfort through the words of David in the Psalms as we moved from place to place. I had called out to God from my knees with countless tears throughout those long fearful days. I had trusted and truly believed that God would deliver us from the evil that threatened to destroy our family. I even praised Him and was faithful to Him for those three months. But the day I came home to an empty house everything changed.

I was convinced that God hated me, and I determined to have nothing to do with such a cruel Master. He had let me down. My soul felt as dead as the brittle Christmas pine needles littering the floor of our living room.

At the time, when I felt the injustice of it all so profoundly, it was difficult to be thankful for anything. The details of the judge's ruling in our case were a first for someone accused of Munchausen and nothing short of a miracle. However, the fact that God had provided a safe, Christian home for our son and that we could visit him daily could not overshadow my feelings. The thought, *Life is just too hard,* reverberated through my head hundreds of times a day, as I attempted to mask my pain from those who might judge me as an unfit mother. Those were dark days.

My twenty-seventh birthday was coming soon. The only gift I wanted was to go to bed knowing my son slept in the room adjacent to mine, snuggled with his kitty in his own bed. Ultimately, the truth of our innocence and yet another positive, thorough psychological evaluation satisfied the judge. After three-and-a-half weeks of separation, our attorney had the privilege of hearing me shout for joy at the news that my son would be coming home. Miracle of miracles: On the day of my birthday Caleb came home. We celebrated his joyous homecoming with about sixty others in our tiny little house that March night.

Even though our little one was home, it was still another month before Seth and I were cleared of all accusations and free to pick up the pieces of our lives. For months afterwards Caleb still would not let me leave the room without panicking. Because of the memory of the unexpected visit from the caseworker, an instant look of fear crossed between us whenever we heard the doorbell but were not expecting visitors. The scars remained fresh for years.

The most significant scar for me though was not emotional; it was spiritual. Those events cemented in my mind the false notion that God did not love me. In God's mercy, He did restore me to Himself in time, but a pervasive sense of mistrust lingered.

Seeking Help

As a result, eight years later, when I found myself living the life of an invalid with nothing but time passed in physical pain, the emotional pain of the earlier tragedy resurfaced. I then realized that I was emotionally and spiritually bankrupt. I finally decided to seek the perspective of a Christian counselor.

Wisely, the counselor discerned the root of my struggles even though I was unaware of it at the time. She pointed out that I did not seem to trust God's Word as true and applicable to me when it spoke words of love. Not surprisingly, I believed God's Word in the hard teachings but overlooked the countless passages in which God affirmed His love for me.

Although I had spent years suffering and searching for answers, the counselor's insight made me realize the true crux of my struggle. It went far deeper than the frequently asked question concerning WHY God allows pain. The heart of the struggle was that, because of my pain, I felt unloved by God and therefore could not trust Him. Until this central issue was resolved, all other attempts at coming to grips with my suffering became temporary fixes at best.

The revelation that I mistrusted God's heart and my counselor's challenge to search for Bible passages that speak of God's love, led me to a short but powerful prayer found in Ephesians 3. With determination, I chose to trust the truth of Ephesians 3:16-21, even though I did not understand it. So began months of meditation, prayer, and contemplation on those inspired words. That prayer launched a transforming journey to understanding God's love for me when some of the events of my life indicated otherwise.

Trusting God's heart is an area that many Christians wrestle with because of the hard blows life has dealt them. It is easy, probably even natural, to either openly or subconsciously hold God responsible for pain and suffering. Perhaps, like me, you "trust" Him as long as He works things out to your liking, but then find yourself disillusioned when He does not. Is that really trust? Do you find it difficult to accept, as I did, that God truly loves you when He allows pain to enter your life?

Songs of God's amazing love ring out in churches all over the world every Sunday. Surely everyone accepts the truth of those words. After all, the first song children learn to sing in Sunday school is *Jesus Loves Me*. Many church-goers struggle endlessly in their walk with the Lord, not realizing that the reason for this stems from their deep-rooted sense that God loves everyone but them. I too was one of those people.

The following chapters reveal the miraculous means of my transformation. No longer are my trials stacking up as evidence against the love of God. Instead, they bear witness to His true character. The truth of the Bible and God's power ended the devastating thought patterns that had long held me captive spiritually and emotionally. My loving Savior took me from the pit of despair and raised me up, so that I can join with King David in saying,

Be at rest once more, O my soul, for the LORD has been good to you. For you, O LORD, have delivered my soul from death, my eyes from tears, my feet from stumbling, that I may walk before the LORD in the land of the living (Ps.116:7-9).[1]

There was hope for me, and there is hope for you as well, so read on.

---

[1] I will use the NIV throughout unless otherwise designated.

Struggle

CHAPTER 2

Tools for the Journey

...to be made new in the attitude of your minds
(Ephesians 4:23)

Have you ever known someone who had a profound impact on your life? Reverend Bob Sizelove, a remarkable man, became such a person for me. When I met him at almost seventy, he bench-pressed two hundred pounds and regularly ran through the red rock hills of Sedona, Arizona for an hour and a half without stopping. Although his age was heard in the timbre of his voice, energy punctuated his every word. One would never guess that during his younger years, overwhelming health problems required him to give up the pastorate. At seventy, however, when not visiting a host of grandkids, the bulk of his days were spent performing weddings and mentoring people like me. Bob's insightful perspective on life in light of Scripture always left me with pearls of wisdom to consider for days to come.

He taught me ways to apply biblical principles that led to experiencing the abundant Christian life.

The abundant Christian life—such a concept used to be a conundrum to me. For most of my life I longed for that supposed abundance, but never succeeded in finding more than momentary happiness. Either God's Word falsely portrayed the Christian life as being full of peace, love and joy, or I was separated, by what I did not know, from God's priceless gifts. Knowing in my heart that the problem was with me, I sought for a solution to that separation.

During one mentoring session, Bob asked me to make a list of things that cause me stress. After a time of contemplating my various stressors, he told me to circle anything that I thought God could not handle. (I encourage you to do the same.) As I looked over the items, the realization hit me. Not a single thing on my list was too big for God. The God who spoke the world into existence could handle anything I faced. More importantly, I **knew** that He could be trusted to work out each situation in the most loving manner possible. Wow! The fact that God managed to bring me to such a simple trust in Him still astounds me.

After Bob and I discussed my firm belief that God could handle any of my stressors, he asked me a rhetorical question. *Then why are you worried?* The proverbial light flickered and then shone brightly—if I truly believe that God is sovereign and out of His unfailing love will do the very best for me, I have no cause for worry. Trusting God is not checking my brain at the door and convincing my emotions to be quiet. It is simply *knowing* I am in good hands.

How many times have you heard pastors or well-meaning encouragers quote **Romans 8:28**? (*And we know that all things work together for good to them that love God, to them who are the called according to his purpose* [KJV].) For those who find it difficult to trust God and believe that He *is* loving, this verse seems to mock rather than comfort. Just think about it: If we could grasp God's incredible love for us, we would handle trials with confidence because of the truth found in Romans 8:28—that God is completely good and sovereign.

God's love is paramount. We must come to a place where we can look at our pain and see God's hand of love, not destruction. Only then, certain that He will lovingly work out *all things* for our good, can we fully rest in Him.

Another common cause for struggle in viewing God as a loving Father and as worthy of trust is a poor or nonexistent relationship with an earthly father. This immense problem deserves its own chapter, but for now I just want to acknowledge this all too frequent cause for mistrusting God. If such is the case with you, please read on.

Regardless though of the specific reasons for wrestling with accepting your heavenly Father's deep love for you and trusting Him accordingly, hope still abounds.

In God's faithfulness He provides powerful tools for ending the separation caused by mistrust, opening the door to the abundant Christian life.

Crossing the Chasm of Mistrust

During the summer of 2009, our family took an unforgettable journey out West. I remember standing on the edge of the Grand Canyon and seeing moving dots at its base. Those dots were people who had hiked the arduous journey to the bottom and at some point would climb out again, victorious. Being a flatlander myself, I struggled for air just climbing the steps to the lookouts along the rim of the canyon. It was hard to imagine the difficulty in crossing that vast chasm, but many do it.

Figuratively speaking, trials and pain often create a chasm of mistrust that separates us from God. Although this separation might include keeping one from salvation itself, I am primarily referring to a separation that causes a Christian to question God's unfailing love. This doubt manifests itself in mistrust, which separates us from a life of lasting joy, peace, and love. Although difficult, with God's power the elimination of deeply ingrained mistrust is possible.

Preparation for a difficult journey across a literal canyon generally requires two things. The first is the most difficult and the one that often prevents people from ever making a challenging expedition. Training! This requires discipline and lots of effort. If someone lacks energy and self-confidence, the training is likely to never begin. Thankfully, God does not require training before the struggling Christian can take that first step across the chasm of mistrust. The only preparation necessary for beginning the journey towards trust is to meet the second and easier of the two requirements. Get outfitted! Near most outdoor adventure sites reside outfitting companies who will provide gear for patrons to successfully conquer the elements. A hiker about to cross the Grand Canyon must acquire proper shoes for hiking and all appropriate equipment.

So also, anyone who figuratively hopes to surmount the chasm of mistrust must be properly outfitted. **2 Corinthians 10:4** tells us that God provides spiritual outfitting, which includes two tools that are not of this world. *On the contrary, they have divine power to demolish strongholds.* The right tools make the crossing possible. The biblical tools of meditating on God's Word and praying enable one to conquer the chasm of mistrust. You can take that first step in the crossing today by taking advantage of these spiritual tools.

The Tool of Meditation

The first tool necessary on the path towards change is meditation. The word *meditation* often causes Christians to cringe because of its associations with yoga and eastern meditation. However, it is a biblical discipline mentioned throughout Scripture. Meditation, very simply put, means *contemplation*, and requires the focusing of one's attention.

Although eastern and biblical meditations are similar in that they both require focused, prolonged contemplation, they are polar opposites in method and goals. The eastern practice is to silence and still oneself so that all negative energy can be released. Peace through *emptying* becomes the goal. In contrast, the biblical practice is to silence and still oneself so that the mind can be *filled* with God's truth. The believer achieves a transformed mind that finds joy and peace in God's presence.

God's Word clearly teaches throughout that what you think and feel determines how you act. Scripture teaches *that out of the overflow of the heart the mouth speaks.*[2] Notice also what **Romans 8:5-6** says about the control of the mind: ***Those who live according to the sinful nature have their minds set on what that nature desires; but those who live in accordance with the Spirit have their minds set on what the Spirit desires....the mind controlled by the Spirit is life and peace.***

For example, do you find that you frequently think fearful or anxious thoughts? Those thoughts are inconsistent with God's countless promises in Scripture. You may not even realize it, but your mind is choosing to

---

[2] Matthew 12:34b

believe the lies of the Deceiver. The end results are choices based on fear and a lack of *life and peace*. As **Psalm 37:8** says, *Do not fret—it leads only to evil.*

How do you change evil behavior? First, you identify what is motivating it—your thinking. Then, you repent. Did you know that the Greek word *repent* translated literally means, *to think differently?*[3] You cannot change your behavior unless you first repent of your wrong thinking. In order to change your wrong thinking, you meditate on God's truth.

I am a doer. If something needs doing, just tell me what is expected, and I will work myself to death trying to achieve the goal. This characteristic might prove useful in many circumstances but works against me spiritually. God calls this striving. God wants me to rest in Him, not strive endlessly to do what only He can do. In the past, when I recognized a pattern of sin in my life I determined to change. Then a cycle began. Try hard to do what is right, fail, feel terrible, repent, and then try again. The results were depressing because I focused on the behavior instead of the wrong thinking behind the behavior.

Do you remember what one gains when a mind is set on what the Spirit desires? Not striving. Life and peace. Do you lack life and peace? Then your thinking is not controlled by the Spirit. By meditating on God's truth you demolish Satan's lies or *arguments and every pretension*

---

[3] Strong's Exhaustive Concordance of the Bible #3340

that sets itself up against the knowledge of God.[4] Meditation repatterns your thought processes. It takes time, but once your thoughts align with God's truth, your behavior naturally changes. Meditation transforms.

Practicing Biblical Meditation

Most people know the familiar lotus position of eastern meditation, but the average Christian finds it difficult to picture the actual practice of biblical meditation. As odd as it may sound, a cow eats in a manner that proves useful as a picture of the process for biblical meditation.

I am always amused when I see cows standing nonchalantly in a field, chewing, while it pours rain. Nothing seems to bother them as long as they can chew the cud all day. They truly are the epitome of peace and calm. Eating for a cow is an all day affair. (Please bear with me as I give details of a cow's digestion, as the details are necessary for the analogy.) First, cows chew grass just enough to swallow, at which time it enters the first stomach. There the stomach partially digests the food, forming the cud, which is then sent back to the mouth for round two. Without hurry, the cow then chews some more before swallowing it again. This time the cud passes into the second stomach. Here the moisture is extracted before the cud is sent back to the mouth again for even more

---
[4] 2 Corinthians 10:5

chewing. This process continues all day until the cud reaches the fourth and final stomach section, where it is finally digested. Unbelievably, a cow chews about eight hours a day or approximately 30,000 chews! Keep that fact in mind as you consider meditating on God's Word.

The practice of biblical meditation corresponds with a cow chewing its cud in many regards. To demonstrate the correlations, I will share the method of meditation that I find effective. Simply, take the principles from my example and tailor the method to meet your circumstances.

The day begins. Because it is easy to be distracted by my own *pressing* thoughts, I begin my devotions by stilling my spirit and praying briefly. (Remember, meditation requires focus.) I simply pray the words of **Psalm 119:18 & 27.** *Open my eyes that I may see wonderful things in your law. Let me understand the teaching of your precepts; then I will meditate on your wonders.*

Afterwards, I read a passage of Scripture and consider its meaning. My goal is to have God speak to me about whatever *He knows* that I need to hear. Therefore, no pre-determined agenda for reading a certain amount is in place. I just thoughtfully read God's Word until something jumps out at me. If I find my mind wandering, I may reread the same section over again until my attention is focused. Then at some point while reading, a phrase or verse(s) grabs my attention. This first reading is like the cow chewing his food just enough to swallow. Unfortunately, this is often where Christians stop. Although benefit comes any time God's Word is read, I eagerly move on to the next step knowing that more riches await me. Having discovered a passage that jumped out at me, I then read it through several more times, contemplating it. Cross referencing similar passages or possibly even reading what others have to say in a commentary may occur at this point as well. Most importantly though, I pray for God's understanding and then allow Him time to direct my thoughts as I silently ponder His Word. This is like the cow on round two of chewing where the juice is extracted. At this point, through the *mind of Christ,*[5] I begin to see insights I never recognized before. I gain new understanding. Suddenly Scripture becomes exciting as I sense God speaking specifically to me.

As incredible as this part is, I am not even close to being done. If I stop there, the new understanding does not have time to weave itself into the fabric of my mind. The activities of the day inevitably redirect my thoughts and prevent lasting, transforming change. After all, I still have 15,000 chews to go!

Next, I write the phrase or verse(s) on a card so that I can carry it with me or place it in a key location in order to memorize and contemplate the Scripture throughout the day. At this point, I am no longer having my devotions but

---

[5] 1 Corinthians 2:16

going about my daily activities. As I memorize that passage of Scripture, my brain processes the truth of God's Word and how it applies to me. This is like the cow's third chewing. The hiding of God's Word in our hearts is essential to countering the lies of the devil.[6] Even Jesus quoted Scripture in the throes of temptation.[7] Tremendous power lies in God's Word!

Finally, I repeat the passage so many times while personalizing it, that the internalized truth begins to affect my actions. This last step may take place over a period of days, weeks, or even months. When I first felt God speaking to me about the depths of His unfailing love for me, I studied and memorized one passage for almost three months. This entire process is what we call meditation. It is a powerful tool God gave us to *demolish strongholds* of any kind, including a lack of trust in God's loving control.

The Tool of Prayer

The second spiritual tool for the journey is prayer, which naturally partners with meditation. While thinking about and internalizing Scripture, I should also be praying it. I claim God's truth for myself, praise and thank Him for it, and ask Him for His power to make it real in my life. **Philippians 2:13** says, *For it is God who works in you to*

---

[6] Psalm 119:11
[7] Luke 4:1-13

will and to act according to his good purpose. We can try all we want to overcome the stronghold of mistrust, but we succeed only if God works supernaturally in us. Therefore, the tool of prayer is crucial.

Jesus, our perfect example, frequently stole away from the crowds and activity to pray. **Luke 5:16** says, *But Jesus often withdrew to lonely places and prayed.* **Mark 1:35** says, *Very early in the morning, while it was still dark, Jesus got up, left the house and went off to a solitary place, where he prayed.* Keep in mind that if anyone ever had pressing work, the Son of God certainly did. There were people to heal, sermons to deliver, and disciples to teach. In spite of the importance of the day's activities, Jesus knew that prayer was essential. God in the Flesh gave up sleep and told people *no* in order to have time to plead with His Father for supernatural help and to maintain fellowship. We must do the same.

Frequently, we grow discouraged with prayer when we do not see definitive answers. **1John 5:14-15** says, *This is the assurance we have in approaching God: that if we ask anything according to his will, he hears us. And if we know that he hears us—whatever we ask—we know that we have what we asked of him.* Now, I cannot vouch for all of your prayers being *according to his will.* I do, however, know that it is most certainly God's will that you grasp His incredible love for you. Therefore, if you struggle with mistrust and doubt that God loves you personally, pray that He will open your eyes to His truth.

He promises to give you this request. The remainder of this book will detail a God given prayer from Ephesians 3 that I strongly recommend making your daily meditation and prayer.

Summary

Let us now go back to the illustration of crossing the chasm of mistrust. Most everyone knows the immensity of the Grand Canyon. Imagine the impossibility of making the hike in flip flops and without drinking water. What would be the chance of success? Similarly, if either of the biblical tools of meditation or prayer is missing, you jeopardize your arduous journey towards change. *But the man who looks intently into the perfect law that gives freedom and continues to do this, not forgetting what he has heard, but doing it—will be blessed in what he does.*"[8] Rely on God's power manifested through His Word and prayer, and you will surmount the cliffs of mistrust and firmly grasp the love of God. The abundant Christian life is within reach. Press on, dear one.

---

[8] James 1:25

CHAPTER 3

Introducing a Transforming Prayer

For this reason I kneel before the Father
(Ephesians 3:14)

A profound prayer in Ephesians 3:16-21 holds a key to true peace, love, and joy. The remainder of this book unfolds the transforming truth found in those verses. Because this prayer focuses on knowing the magnitude of God's love, I call it the Love Prayer. It takes the struggle of grasping the love of God to the Lord himself, who alone is capable of opening our eyes and allowing us to see His immense love. Scriptures on the love of God abound, but the Ephesians passage uniquely combines truth meditation in the form of a prayer, thereby, making use of both our God-given tools at one time.[9]

---

[9] The tools of prayer & meditation were discussed in ch.2.

The apostle Paul authored the Love Prayer. Oddly enough, this great apostle appears to be someone targeted to suffer greatly. Surely our sufferings pale in comparison with his. While spreading the Good News of Jesus Christ, Paul was imprisoned multiple times, flogged near to death eight times, stoned and left for dead, shipwrecked and afloat at sea for a day and a night, homeless, constantly in danger, not to mention being deprived at times of sleep, food, water, and clothes. Yikes! That would be enough to discourage anyone, and yet somehow it did not affect Paul negatively.[10] Why?

As I meditated on Paul's inspired words in the Love Prayer, I asked myself repeatedly how someone who suffered as he did still managed to grasp God's love. The passion and depth with which Paul felt the love of God dominates the beautiful Ephesians prayer. What did he see that I missed? He obviously felt God's love deeply in spite of his tremendous suffering, as can be seen throughout his prolific writings in the New Testament. Furthermore, he desperately wanted all believers to grasp God's amazing love as he did.

In the fourteen verses introducing the prayer, we find several clues that explain Paul's perspective on God's love in the midst of suffering. We also discover a well-laid foundation, which enables us to understand the prayer's significance. So, before we dive into the life-changing

---

[10] II Corinthians 11:23-29

waters of the prayer itself, it is important that we understand this framework. In one portion, the apostle Paul said,

> *In reading this, then, you will be able to understand my insight into the mystery of Christ....This mystery is that through the gospel the Gentiles are heirs together with Israel, members together of one body, and sharers together in the promise in Christ Jesus* (vv. 4-6).

What is this *mystery*? It is not that the Gentiles would be saved, since the Old Testament already allowed for that. Instead, it is that they form one body of Christ equal and together with the Jews. Because you probably already know about the equality of the Jews and Gentiles in Christ, you may not understand why Paul says that being a joint or co-heir is a mystery. Perhaps you take this status for granted. Paul, on the other hand, did not and had reasons for emphasizing this status before his prayer.

An Illustration from Ancient Rome

To give perspective, let me tell you of an unusual occurrence in ancient Roman history that illustrates the remarkableness of the privilege of being a joint-heir. At a time when the Roman Empire still ruled the world but was beginning to lose its stronghold to the barbarians, a man known as Hadrian ruled the Empire. In 136 AD Emperor Hadrian, then sixty, turned his thoughts to who would succeed him in power, since he had no son. Many in Rome desired this coveted position of power.

Hadrian, however, contrived to manipulate a man of his own choosing into the position of emperor upon his death. A simple adoption of the man of his choosing was all that was necessary. Unfortunately, his well-laid plan fell apart when two years later his adopted son died of poor health, while Hadrian still reigned.

Enter Antoninus Pius. Having inherited the wealth of both of his grandfathers, Antoninus was one of the richest men in Rome at the time and a respected senator. By the time he turned fifty-two, he had gained quite a reputation under Emperor Hadrian. Antoninus, like the emperor, had no sons of his own.

After the failure of Hadrian's first plan, the emperor devised a more elaborate and outrageous scheme. Tongues surely wagged across Rome at the news. The emperor's plan first required the adoption of Antoninus, who would in turn adopt two specific sons: Marcus Aurelius and Lucius.

The multiple adoptions proved necessary because Hadrian's preferred choices for emperor were too young to rule for a number of years yet. Marcus Aurelius was sixteen, and Lucius was still just a boy. Antoninus, on the other hand, at fifty-two seemed old by Roman standards. Therefore, Hadrian assumed, Antoninus would only rule briefly while the adopted sons matured. Surprisingly, this "aged" ruler reigned for twenty-three years after Hadrian died. The final, most outlandish detail of the scheme specified that the two adopted sons should one day be co-emperors.

Meanwhile, Antoninus Pius' two adopted sons made names for themselves in the Roman Empire. Years passed. Regardless of Hadrian's dying wishes, all of Rome expected Marcus Aurelius, being the older and first adopted son, to be the next emperor. Aurelius' upbringing was clearly a grooming for the emperorship, while Lucius' upbringing was not. To further strengthen Aurelius' claim as heir, Antoninus gave his daughter to be Aurelius' bride. Upon the emperor's death in 161 A.D., Aurelius, having a double claim as heir to the thrown by adoption and marriage, rightfully inherited the role of emperor.

Now before I tell the surprise ending, keep in mind the desperate attempts to gain and keep power, which permeate every nation in history. Throughout all of ancient Roman history, one man after another attempted to gain the power afforded an emperor and murdered anyone who stood in his way. Mothers murdered sons, and sons murdered their mothers. Brothers murdered brothers. Emperors murdered entire families without hesitation to guarantee that no rival replaced them as emperor of the mighty Roman Empire.

In the midst of this cut-throat culture, the good and generous Marcus Aurelius did something shocking. Following the death of Antoninus Pius, Aurelius offered three things to his adopted brother, Lucius. The first was a name change/addition for Lucius that would forever link him to their adoptive father. Secondly, Aurelius generously offered an equal share in the inheritance of their father's vast riches. Lastly and most surprising of all, he willingly offered to become co-emperors with the newly named Lucius Verus. For the first time there were two emperors in Rome. For nine years the two shared the rule and riches of the greatest empire up to that time.

The idea of such a thing would have been considered a *mystery* to all in the land. How the shocking news would have spread across the empire like wildfire! Both men were adopted by a generous benefactor, but only one was expected to be the heir. Instead, the brothers became equals, sharing everything Rome had to offer.

Similar to Roman culture, Jewish culture allowed that only the firstborn gain the maximum benefits as the primary heir. However, God, our generous benefactor, also had an *outlandish* plan. Unlike Hadrian, God did have a rightful heir, Jesus, and yet He still chose and adopted, first the Jews and then the Gentiles. (It is also interesting to note that God has given us His name and will one day have us marry into His family as well.)

History tells us that Lucius Verus thoroughly enjoyed the privilege of being joint-heir and all of the blessings of such a status. We to, as co-heirs to God's throne, enjoy untold privileges in this life as well as the life to come. Our status gives us the privilege of direct access to *the unsearchable riches of Christ* (Ephesians 3:8). Could understanding our position as heirs, be the starting point for grasping the love of God? Paul certainly thought so.

The Privilege of Direct Access

Continuing on in the introduction, we find one of the *riches* of our status as Paul goes into more detail a few verses later: ***In him and through faith in him we may approach God with freedom and confidence.***[11] Prayer is how we approach the Almighty God. Paul wanted to remind us, before he began the Love Prayer, of what an awesome privilege it is to have direct access to God at any time.

I remember a poignant scene in the modern movie version of The King and I, when the King of Siam is seated on his throne at the end of a vast and opulent hall. Dignitaries stand below him discussing important matters of the kingdom. The setting is rife with pomp and circumstance. Suddenly, a young waif of a girl, visibly upset, barges through a door at the back of the hall. Although dwarfed by her surroundings, this child boldly rushes past the dignified men and unceremoniously jumps into the king's lap. The dignitaries' jaws drop open.

---

[11] Ephesians 3:12

Without showing any frustration or anger at the presumption of the child to interrupt his important business, the king immediately and tenderly gives the little one his full attention. This child was correct in assuming, with complete confidence, that the king would lovingly help her in her time of need. Why? Because of course, she is his daughter--a child of the king.

That scene depicts the picture Paul conveys when he says God's children can enter the throne room of the King of the Universe with *freedom and confidence*. God is never too busy to lovingly respond in our time of need. God avails this incredible privilege to Jews and Gentiles alike, as joint-heirs, through faith in the shed blood of Christ. So, before the Love Prayer begins, Paul reminds his readers of the tremendous mystery and benefit of our position in Christ.

The Problem of Suffering

The very next verse in the introduction, however, is quite unexpected at first glance. *I ask you, therefore, not to be discouraged because of my sufferings for you, which are your glory* (Eph. 3:13). At first this verse seems random, but it is not. Do not forget, all of Paul's recorded thoughts came from the inspiration of the Holy Spirit. The apostle purposefully interjected the topic of suffering after spending twelve verses focusing on the privilege of being a child of God and immediately before the Love Prayer begins. We must assume that a connection exists between the three topics of this passage--our position before God, suffering, and the Love Prayer. Why does Paul view the privilege of complete access to God as a cause for encouragement when it did not bring relief from his problems? Why is that not cause for more discouragement rather than hope?

Paul found tremendous encouragement in his position as a child of the King because God gave him extraordinary insight into the incredible value of that position. Being an heir of God provided everything he needed for this world and, more importantly, a future hope that would never disappoint. His focus shifted from self to God, from the seen to the unseen, from the temporary to the eternal. In 1 **Corinthians 4:17** Paul describes that shift in perspective.

> *For our light and momentary troubles are achieving for us an eternal glory that far outweighs them all. So we fix our eyes not on what is seen, but what is unseen. For what is seen is temporary but what is unseen is eternal.*

Paul's perspective on his sufferings was radically changed. Now, I am not suggesting, nor is the apostle, that this shift in perspective is the starting place for those struggling with suffering. Although many books on pain begin with the need to change to an eternal perspective, this book will not. The believer's perspective naturally changes as a result of grasping the infinite love of Christ. This change cannot be forced into place with any lasting effect. I want to deal with the root of the problem; i.e. mistrust due to feeling unloved by God. This book does not further the guilt of those suffering by placing demands that are unattainable.

Paul knew his own sufferings might be discouraging to believers, so he introduced the prayer by acknowledging them. He understood that suffering frequently causes problems with the way we view God. It becomes difficult to comprehend God's blessings in light of suffering, unless we too can gain deep insight and perspective like Paul. This insight and the peace and joy it brings only comes from God and is otherwise unattainable. Out of this understanding, the apostle penned a profound prayer.

The Significance of Kneeling

Let us now consider one final, yet significant phrase found in Paul's introduction to the Love Prayer. The heartfelt phrase that comes immediately before the Love Prayer showed Paul's grasp on the difficulty of trusting God's love in the midst of suffering. He simply said, *For this reason I kneel before the Father* (vs. 14).

Many think that kneeling was commonplace in the Bible and therefore, miss the significance of Paul's simple phrase. Actually, the Bible mentions any number of postures for praying. With only a couple of exceptions, Bible characters reserved kneeling for times of dire need, such as when Hannah fell on her knees to beg God for a son or when Jesus prayed in the Garden of Gethsemane. The mention of kneeling here indicates the apostle's belief that the need for God's people to experience the blessings of the Love Prayer is so crucial, so dire, and so necessary, that he fell to his knees to pray it. That is the setting of the inspired words to come.

God worked the words of this prayer into my heart and soul, freeing me from doubts and fears. No longer does the ravenous shark circle in the waters of my thoughts. This work only God can do, and I pray that as you read this book, the loving Savior changes how you think and feel about His loving kindness as well.

The Love Prayer

"I pray that out of his glorious riches he may strengthen you with power through his Spirit in your inner being, so that Christ may dwell in your hearts through faith.

And I pray that you, being rooted and established in love, may have power, together with all the saints, to grasp how wide and long and high and deep is the love of Christ, and to know this love that surpasses knowledge— that you may be filled to the measure of all the fullness of God.

Now to him who is able to do immeasurably more than all we ask or imagine, according to his power that is at work within us, to him be glory in the church and in Christ Jesus throughout all generations, for ever and ever! Amen."

Ephesians 3:16-21

Part 2

Power

Power

CHAPTER 4

Inward Power

*I pray that out of his glorious riches he may
strengthen you with power through his Spirit in your
inner being* (Ephesians 3:16).

[12]Have you heard the joke about the African-American pastor in a small, country church on the back roads of Mississippi? Well, the story goes like this: A well-meaning pastor wanted to illustrate to his poor congregation a sermon on prayer and God's endless riches. In a moment of creativity, the preacher made arrangements with a local boy, for what he was certain was a divinely inspired illustration. The lad was to climb up into the attic that opened over the stage near the pulpit before church began Sunday morning. Sworn to secrecy, the youth was armed with a sack of potatoes and instructed to quietly wait

---

[12]If you have not already taken the time to carefully read the prayer on the preceding page in its entirety, please do so before you read any further.

in the attic during the service for his cue. Only then was he to individually drop the potatoes from the opening.

With tremendous passion, the preacher expounded upon several Scriptures telling how God's people should cry out to God in times of need. The good Lord will then faithfully answer out of His abundant riches, the pastor assured his congregation. All was going according to plan, and shouts of *Amen brother!* and *You preach it pastor!* reverberated off the wooden walls of the church.

The moment for the lad's cue had come. *You say you ain't got 'nough to feed yo' family. Well, cry out to God fo' potaters, and He's sure ta provide em!* With arms held up high and head up-lifted, he went on to shout, *Lawd, give us some potaters!* and a couple of potatoes fell from the ceiling.

The congregation responded in unison with gasps of amazement. Being spurred on by their response, the pastor continued on with increasing fervor and gesticulations to beg the *Good Lord* for more potatoes. After several minutes of these impassioned pleas, which accounted for a host of potatoes strewn across the stage, a small head appeared upside-down from the attic opening.

The small boy shouted out, *The Lawd ain't got no mo' potaters!*

Thankfully, unlike the preacher's sermon illustration gone awry in the joke, true prayer directed towards the LORD of the Universe remains powerful and effective. Don't forget, the biblical tool of prayer enables you to cross the chasm of mistrust. The Love Prayer begins with two simple words that state the uniqueness of what is to follow: "I pray."

A Personal Prayer

Numerous prayers fill the pages of the Bible. Although some of them demonstrate an individual's personal plea to the Almighty, some, like the Lord's Prayer and the Love Prayer, provide powerfully inspired petitions that believers should utilize. The apostle Paul prayed the Love Prayer on behalf of all Believers, but intended for Christians to make it their personal prayer as well. I encourage you to choose a time of the day during which you will thoughtfully and routinely pray the Love Prayer. Whether it is during your devotions, before you go to bed at night, or some other time of your choosing makes no difference. Because prayer is a powerful tool, the simple act of praying this inspired prayer from the heart can bring dramatic changes in your heart and mind. I know it has in mine.[13]

If you do not yet understand the depth of meaning in the words of this prayer, do not be concerned. God does. The pages ahead give powerful understanding, one phrase at a time, to this incredible passage. Meanwhile, God in his

---

[13] To make simple this transition from general to personal, the Love Prayer (Ephesians 3:16-21) can be found at the book's end with all pronouns changed to first person.

awesome power faithfully works as you daily seek Him using Paul's inspired words. My desire is that, while reading the chapters of this book, you meditate on the life changing truth you learn. Then the tool of meditation joins with the tool of prayer to bring about a transformation at which you will marvel.

A Request for Strength

Having read the Love Prayer, you know that its purpose lies in the believer knowing and grasping the magnitude of God's love. However, the apostle Paul does not immediately jump into that request because prerequisites come first for one to truly grasp God's amazing love. So instead, Paul begins this prayer with, *I pray that out of his glorious riches he may strengthen you with power through his Spirit in your inner being* **(Eph. 3:16a).** Yes, spiritual strength and power are requisite for truly knowing the love of God.

Having gone through nineteen years of health problems, I understand the need for God's strengthening power to make it through life's responsibilities. However, the request for strength that starts off the Love Prayer centers in the spirit, not the body. Through this first request, we once again see that the apostle understood the tremendous difficulty people have in grasping the love of God. He knew we must have God's strength to move forward in trust!

Strengthened with the Spirit's power

Two Greek words work in conjunction to form this beginning request. The first word, *strengthen*, means *to empower, increase in vigor, be strengthened.*[14] The second word, *power*, or *dunamis* in the Greek, means *specifically miraculous power (usually by implication, a miracle itself)...*[15]

Although just a brief prayer of six verses, the Love Prayer mentions power three times. The New Testament frequently uses this meaning of the word in reference to two things: God's power itself or God's power manifested in believers for His glory. Both are miraculous indeed!

How do believers in Jesus Christ gain the miraculous power of inner strengthening that enables us to know and grasp the love of God? At the moment of placing faith in Christ alone for salvation, the Holy Spirit enters into the Believer's heart (Galatians 4:6). The Spirit then lives in the believer till death or until Christ's return. He then performs numerous tasks, such as empowerment.

Resurrection power

Another passage, **Ephesians 1:19-20** gives a surprising clarification to this *dunamis* power.

---

[14] Strong's Exhaustive Concordance of the Bible #2901.
[15] Strong's Exhaustive Concordance of the Bible #1411.

...and his incomparably great power for us who believe. ***That power is like the working of his mighty strength, which he exerted in Christ when he raised him from the dead and seated him at his right hand in the heavenly realm.***

No one overcomes death! Yet, the Giver of Life used His incomparably great power to raise up Jesus, three days dead and buried. That is miraculous power! Furthermore, those verses say that God makes that same power available to all those who believe.

Paul uses the same Greek word for power, *dunamis,* in every instance found in the Love Prayer. In other words, the miraculous power God used to raise Christ from the dead is the same power we should pray for, first, in order to strengthen us inwardly that we might trust Christ. Secondly, we should again pray for God's miraculous power in order that we might be able to grasp how wide and long and high and deep is the love of Christ (Eph.3:18). Evidently the apostle knew the impossibility for finite humans to fathom the love of an infinite God, so do not underestimate the importance of asking for supernatural power through the Holy Spirit. His power makes possible the grasping of essential nutrients—trust and love—to a malnourished soul.

The ordeal of Truman C. Everts

Let me illustrate with an incredible survival story I learned of in a documentary on Yellowstone National Park. Having witnessed first-hand the landscape of Yellowstone, shaped by multiple, massive volcanic explosions and continued geothermal activity, I marveled at the ordeal of Truman C. Everts.

First of all, you have to understand the size of this beloved place of wild beauty. The park is massive— 3,468.4 square miles and made up of lakes, canyons, forests, mountain ranges, rivers, and the world's largest super volcano. Everywhere you go in the park, hot substances bubble up out of the ground—even in inconvenient places like in the middle of a parking lot. *Half of the world's geothermal features are in Yellowstone, fueled by this ongoing volcanism.*[16] The tremendous quantity and variety of wildlife that roams freely also bears mentioning. In the early days, no roads, trails, visitor centers, or gift shops existed—just wilderness in its most primitive state.

In this setting in the year 1870, Truman C. Everts, at forty-eight years of age, found himself separated from his exploration party. How Everts, an IRS agent, managed to be included in such an adventurous trip remains unclear.

---

[16] http://en.wikipedia.org/wiki/Yellowstone_National _Park#cite_note-geothermal-8

Nevertheless, he was included, and as the group attempted to make its way through dense forest filled with large sections of fallen trees, Everts struck out on his own to find a navigable path. In doing so, he became separated from his group. To make matters significantly worse, the following day his horse, which carried all of his provisions, bolted in fright, leaving the would-be explorer completely alone and unprepared.

Everts describes his trials in "Thirty-seven Days of Peril."

> *Naturally timid in the night, I fully realized the exposure of my condition. I peered upward through the darkness, but all was blackness and gloom. The wind sighed mournfully through the pines. The forest seemed alive with the screeching of night birds, the angry barking of coyotes, and the prolonged, dismal howl of the gray wolf. These sounds, familiar by their constant occurrence throughout the journey, were now full of terror, and drove slumber from my eyelids.*[17]

His story of survival continued on for thirty-six more excruciating days in the wilderness of Upper Yellowstone. One might think that with so much wildlife he would have found or caught enough food to sustain himself. Unfortunately, his story is not one of great skill and knowledge in how to forage or hunt. No, his story

---

[17] Scribner's Monthly Vol.III. November, 1871. No.1, "Thirty-seven Days of Peril"

involved only misfortune and wandering, slowly starving, being badly burnt, treed by a mountain lion, and caught in a snowstorm for days. When two men found him, he weighed a mere fifty pounds. In his own words, Everts describes his rescue.

"God bless him and them and you! I am saved!" *and with these words, powerless of further effort, I fell forward into the arms of my preservers, in a state of unconsciousness. I was saved. On the very brink of the river which divides the known from the unknown, strong arms snatched me from the final plunge, and kind ministrations wooed me back to life.*[18]

Do you think that Everts in his horribly emaciated condition quickly recovered? After being found, he promptly lost consciousness, and it took two days of great care before he could be moved to the nearest cabin twenty miles away. Then, after days of being fed broth, his new friends doubted his recovery. Too much time of malnourishment had passed for his body to return to normal digestion. His physical torment was severe. At this point, a surprise visitor arrived.

An old man in mountain costume entered—a hunter, whose life was spent among the mountains...He, listened to the story of my

---

[18] Ibid

sufferings, and tears rapidly coursed each other down his rough, weather-beaten face. But when he was told of my present necessity, brightening in a moment, he exclaimed:
"Why, Lord bless you, if that is all, I have the very remedy you need. In two hours' time all shall be well with you."[19]

The mountain man was pleased to supply fresh bear fat, and lots of it for Everts' consumption. Sure enough, the following day Everts was again capable of digesting food and his pain was abated.

The illustration explained

Allow me now to make some observations about this story. Digestion should naturally occur. From the time of birth the involuntary action of the digestive system takes place. As food passes through our body, nutrients are absorbed to nourish our bodies and the waste is eliminated.

However, the trauma and severe lack of food that Truman C. Everts endured for thirty-seven days left his normal processes arrested. His kind rescuers provided easy to digest foods in an attempt to slowly restore him to health, but more, something special, was needed. As unlikely as it might seem, it took drinking two cups of liquefied bear fat to jump-start what once came naturally.

---

[19] Ibid

Speaking of what should be natural: Two of the first things an infant learns in life are love and trust. They do not realize it in a conscious sort of way, of course, but when they are held, spoken to, caressed, fed, and cared for they learn life's great lessons. As children grow a little older, if mom and dad are decent parents, children become secure in those lessons. The faith or trust of such a child proves remarkable.

However, as children mature into adults they face the realities of the human condition—depravity, failure, disappointment, and pain. This journey through life's hardness can leave a soul malnourished and unable to process trust in a loving savior. Perhaps you find yourself in that state now. Like the broth administered to Everts in his weakened condition, words like mine might prove mildly helpful but totally insufficient. You just cannot break the patterns of thought ingrained in you. You require something more.

Paul knew what we lack, and he asks for it three times in the Love Prayer—the Holy Spirit's strengthening power. Miraculous power to jump-start what should have been natural—trusting the perfect love of God. Never considering that God's power in us is so mighty, most believers fail to pray for this invaluable resource. This power can make it possible to conquer strongholds in our lives or enable us in whatever manner He sees fit. We need only to pray for it. If the power God supplies His children with is the same power that He used to raise Jesus to life, then it is powerful enough to help anyone grasp the love of God. Begin praying for God's power to trust in a loving Father today.

Strengthen us inwardly.

Now that we know the source and the type of power available to strengthen the Christian, we can look at another aspect of the request. Again Paul says, *I pray that out of his glorious riches he may strengthen you with power through his Spirit **in your inner being*** (Eph.3:16). Take note of the specific location of this strengthening. The strengthening takes place in our *inner being*.

What exactly is this *inner being*? Interestingly, the Love Prayer alone uses the exact phrase, *inner being*. A similar passage gives more detail though. **2 Corinthians 4:16** says, ***For which cause we faint not; but though our outward man perish, yet the inward man is renewed day by day*** (KJV). This indicates that the inner man contrasts with the outward or physical body of man. Paul conveys, therefore, that one experiences the powerful strengthening of the Spirit, not outwardly, but inwardly in the core of our being.

We live in a society where stress has become the routine instead of the exception—a society where people use more time saving conveniences than at any other time in history and yet still long for more hours in the day—a society in which the average person consumes caffeine, pain pills, and other pharmaceuticals at an alarming rate, just to make it through the press of a day's responsibilities. What a relief to know that God awaits your request to strengthen you in the core of your being, where you need it most? Yoga or some other form of inward renewal will not nourish your starving soul. God's power will. You do not have to overcome the struggle to trust God on your own power. Recognize your need and look to the mighty King on His throne for His limitless provision.

CHAPTER 5

The Difficulty with Trust

*I pray that out of his glorious riches he may strengthen you with power through his Spirit in your inner being **so that Christ may dwell in your hearts through faith.***
(Ephesians 3:16-17a)

When my son turned twelve, he happily picked out a dog at the pound for his birthday. After many trips up and down the aisle of dog cages discussing the pros and cons of each, he settled on an adorable Jack Russell Terrier, (Jack Russell *terror,* which we now know many fondly call that particular breed.), and we took him home.

Our new spotted friend was to be an outside-only pet, due in large part to our concern for the well-being of our two long- established indoor cats. Consequently, we began the necessary preparations to ready the yard for the dog's coming. My husband and son spent the entire day, prior to the dog's arrival, finishing a fence. As projects frequently do, the fence's completion took longer than expected, and so, at the close of the day, no doghouse had been constructed. Being first time dog owners, we thought a patio table pulled under the eaves of the house would suffice for one night. Boy, were we wrong!

Needless to say, our new little friend did not feel at home and spent the night camped on our doorstep barking and whining. Clearly, it was not enough to merely invite the dog to our home. We also needed to make the conditions for his dwelling agreeable to permanent, hospitable living.

Bleary-eyed from lack of sleep, the next day I built our furry friend a cozy little doghouse by the back door and put a blanket in it. Thankfully, the soothing night sounds of crickets instead of barking indicated that the dog felt at home, and sleep came to all.

In similar fashion Christ can be made to feel *left out in the cold*. We can invite him to move into our hearts; so to speak, but upon arrival fail to make our hearts places where He feels truly welcome. The next phrase in the Love Prayer addresses one element that makes our hearts suitable dwelling places for Christ.

The reason behind the request

Throughout the last chapter, I explained the first half of the request in the Love Prayer (that God would strengthen us in our inner being). In this chapter I will address the second half of that request for strength, which says, *so that Christ might dwell in our hearts through faith*. The word *so* used in that phrase tells us that the nine words that follow give the purpose or reason for this request for inner strengthening. Understanding the phrase—*so that Christ might dwell in our hearts through faith*--correctly, then, is key to understanding the request for inner strength.

As already mentioned in the last chapter, when people put their faith in Christ alone, the Holy Spirit indwells them. This prayer, however, was written for believers who already have the gift of salvation. Think about it. A true child of God has no need to pray desperately for strength in order to put their faith in Christ for salvation. They already have salvation. Therefore, another, more logical interpretation of the phrase, *so that Christ might dwell in our hearts through faith* must exist.

To find the answer let us consider the original meaning of the word *dwell* used in this verse. It means, *to house permanently...*[20] One commentary offers the following explanation of the words in question: It means, *not merely to live, but to be at home--to abide.... that he may be at home there in the sense that the believer has given over his whole life to him.*[21] When the apostle Paul writes of *Christ dwelling in our hearts through faith* he indicates that faith at all times makes our hearts hospitable

[20] Strong's Exhaustive Concordance of the Bible #2730
[21] The New Testament and Wycliffe Bible Commentary p.737

places for Christ to reside. Just as my new dog required certain things to make our place a suitable home to him, in a spiritual sense, Jesus requires continual faith or trust.

An illustration of faith

Although this verse does not refer to the faith needed for salvation, we can draw parallels from a simple illustration for trust in a tract put out by Evan Tell.[22] It explains that the faith necessary for salvation is like the trust shown every time you sit in a chair. Usually when sitting, you do so without much thought. Since when do you first inspect the chair closely to see if it will hold you before plopping down? Never. Or, once sitting, you would not position your weight forward on your feet as a precaution to ensure that you do not fall if the chair were to collapse. Instead, you sit without hesitation, confident that it will hold you, indicating your unwavering trust in the chair.

When we apply the chair illustration spiritually, we recognize that all reliance on self-effort for salvation, such as good behavior or church attendance, must be removed from our thinking as we unhesitatingly put our trust in Christ alone for salvation. The need for faith, however, does not end after the moment of salvation. Quite the opposite is true! Christ wants that same simple faith to

---

[22] *May I ask you a question?* Dr. Larry Moyer

continue by daily trusting Him to lovingly handle every area of our lives.

Taking the chair analogy a step further, suppose for a moment though that you feel the chair has been kicked out from under you or collapsed one too many times? How do you trust Christ then? For most of my Christian life I had no trouble trusting Christ for salvation but struggled immensely with trusting him to love me and do what was best for me on a daily basis. You may relate but have grown uncomfortably accustomed to the problem, thinking that it cannot be resolved.

Lack of trust makes a home inhospitable

A familiar scenario applies to this spiritual dilemma. Have you ever lived in a home where you were not trusted by someone such as a parent or a spouse? Maybe it was justified, and maybe it was not. Regardless, what was the atmosphere of that home like, and did you consider it a pleasant place to dwell?

When a wife no longer trusts her husband because of his infidelity, she is quick to doubt his word, quick to anger, and quick to find fault with him. His every action or inaction is called into question. She chooses to *handle* things on her own, assuming that he cannot be relied upon. Certainly, hospitable would not be a word used to characterize such a home. For that marriage to survive, the difficult tasks of forgiveness being offered and trust being regained must occur.

Generally speaking in human cases, one person's repeated failures cause pain to another and a lack of trust results. Because God never fails or messes up, when we distrust Him it is because we have been deceived into thinking that God is at fault or does not care. Please do not bail out on me if that statement angers you, but instead take a moment to think about it. Since I will discuss this in greater depth in a later chapter, suffice it to say for now that regardless of the cause, the problem is still the same: past pain can result in distrusting God.

How does that distrust play out in our walk with the Lord? Similar to the injured wife, an injured Christian is quick to doubt God's Word, quick to get angry at God, and quick to find fault with God's plan and blame Him for all hurts. His every action or inaction is called into question. This lack of trust shows itself in a determination to do things our own way. These characteristics make a heart inhospitable to Christ.

Trust is foundational

Did you know that the Bible refers to or commands trust in God over one hundred and thirty-five times and that number does not even include over a hundred other references to faith? Faith or trust forms the foundation of a relationship with Christ, and the sheer number of biblical references indicates its importance.

One such passage is **Isaiah 50:10b** which says, *Let him who walks in the dark, who has no light, trust in the name of the Lord and rely on his God.* Another verse simply describes the state of mind of one walking in the light of faith. *Whoever trusts in the LORD, happy is he (Proverbs 16:20* NKJ). As I once knew all too well, when distrust of the Lord rules a heart, doubts, anger, and fear surface quickly. Perhaps, you can relate.

Trust brings happiness

We all want to be happy but so few are. The divorce rate is sky-rocketing as non-Christians and Christians alike try to find happiness with someone else. After all, we deserve to be happy, right? At one time I would have answered that with an emphatic, "No." What we deserve is death (Romans 6:23). Although true, such a harsh response skews the hard teachings of the Bible and skips right over the loving ones. Surely some balance is needed.

Again, the aforementioned verse from Proverbs says that trust in the Lord produces happiness. Another powerful passage in **Psalm 16** states that because God is before and beside me (notice the proximity to God that implies trust), I will not be shaken and therefore,

*my heart is glad and my tongue rejoices; my body
also will rest secure, because you will not abandon
me to the grave... you will fill me with joy in your
presence, with eternal pleasures at your right hand*
(v 8-11).

Wow! Notice all of the inferred references to trust
in those verses as well as the references to different positive
feelings that are the result of trust in God. In other words,
God does want us to be happy, glad, joyful, rejoicing, at
rest, and experiencing pleasure, but those things come
when we trust God enough to keep him *before and beside*
us. The temporary pleasures of sin that make us "happy"
for a time make a poor substitute for what God has in store
for those who trust in Him.

For many years now my favorite hymn has been,
Tis So Sweet to Trust in Jesus by Louisa M.R. Stead. The
simple words of the first stanza and chorus are,

Tis so sweet to trust in Jesus,
just to take him at His word,
just to rest upon His promise,
just to know, "Thus saith the Lord."
Jesus, Jesus, how I trust Him!
How I've proved Him o'er and o'er!
Jesus, Jesus, precious Jesus!
O for grace to trust Him more![23]

---

[23] William J. Kirkpatrick, 1838-1921 and Louisa M.R. Stead, c.18-50-1917.

I longed, in an almost palpable way, for that kind of faith because I knew the peace and happiness that it would bring. Because I knew the lyrics remained untrue of me, I used to cry, without fail, part way through singing that song. Now, I sometimes still get teary when singing that hymn (Oh, the oddities of being a woman!), but it is because I am utterly amazed that God could so completely change a lifetime of distrust. God can do the impossible!

If you have had the proverbial chair crash out from under you a time or two, you likely know what a struggle it is to trust Christ enough to give him full reign in your life. Trust seems elusive because you are brokenhearted--held captive by hurt, disappointment and anger. You desperately need release from the chair-kicked-out-from-under-you syndrome, which keeps one from trusting Christ fully. What is to be done for those who grapple with this issue? Well, the apostle Paul recognized this immense obstacle and prayed for us on bended knee to have miraculous, inward power to recognize the love of God and to trust fully in Him as a result. I find that enormously encouraging!

Help is on the way

I have read and heard people say; *Just trust in God,* as if a person can simply blink their eyes like the actress in I Dream of Jeannie and poof, trust appears. Think for example, of children who have been physically abused and consequently have developed a reflex to shield their faces when someone raises a hand towards them. Can the patterns deeply ingrained in their brains be immediately erased just because a kind and caring individual suddenly steps into their lives? No, it takes time and patient love to repattern their thinking and responses. Yet, in similar fashion, Christians often expect instant trust in God from individuals who have many reasons to question His trustworthiness.

Thankfully, one can find proof in Scripture that God both understands this struggle, and offers true hope for the believer who wrestles with these issues. **Isaiah 61:1** says,

> *The Spirit of the sovereign Lord is on me, because the Lord has anointed me to preach good news to the poor. He has sent me to bind up the brokenhearted, to proclaim freedom for the captives and release for the prisoners.*

Over 750 years after the time that Isaiah prophesied those words, Luke 4 describes Jesus reading that very passage aloud during a Sabbath service in a synagogue in Nazareth.

Just picture the scene. Jesus, with an air of authority in his voice and yet a humble demeanor, begins to read from the scroll of Isaiah to a crowd of men curious to hear what the famed Nazarene has to say. After reading, He silently rolls up the scroll and declares to a hushed crowd; t*oday this scripture is fulfilled in your hearing* (v 21).

This claim to be the fulfillment of an ancient prophecy was no small thing. However, Christ's earthly ministry did fulfill it perfectly. Caring deeply for hurting people, God set in motion a plan, established thousands of years in advance, to free people from their bonds through Christ. And, according to Paul, the same Holy Spirit that came on Jesus to give Him the power to *bind up the brokenhearted...proclaim freedom for the captive and release for the prisoners* also gives us the power to allow *Christ to dwell in our hearts through faith.*

Do not miss the incredible implications here: Christ came with the anointing of the Spirit so that He might heal and free people to *have life, and...have it more abundantly* (**John 10:10** KJV). God knows we struggle daily with trusting Christ and letting Him abide in our hearts. Unlike the cruel Pharaoh of Moses' time who demanded that the Israelites make the same number of bricks with fewer materials, God instead willingly supplies us with all we need to accomplish the seemingly impossible task of trusting Him. We need only to ask.

Condemning us for our lack of trust would be God's right, but instead, He offers us the necessary tool through his Spirit -- miraculous power to strengthen us inwardly in order that we might, through faith, make our hearts hospitable to Him. We cannot overcome the lack of trust in the blink of an eye or even with great therapy. We need to meditate on the truth of God's Word and pray for this transformation. Why not begin today?

Part 3

Love

CHAPTER 6

Understanding Your Roots

And I pray that you, being rooted and established in love, (Ephesians 3:17b)

The summer of my eighteenth year, I worked as a day camp counselor for six- and seven- year-old boys. We energetically tromped through the woods on nature hikes, played in the pool, constructed craft projects, sang silly songs, and generally exhausted ourselves in the great outdoors. As is typical of kids, the boys frequently surprised me with the things they did. One particular surprise impacted me greatly.

Each day we counselors had a story time with our individual groups for the purpose of teaching *values.* I quickly decided that Bible stories contained the most interesting and effective material for teaching values. Daily, the mostly unchurched boys listened, totally enthralled by my retelling of the adventures of biblical heroes. During this story time, I would take a blanket and spread it out on the grass under a big shade tree, where the boys would sprawl while I animatedly drew them into Bible times.

On one particular hot, summer day, I told my boys the story of Christ's death on the cross, and they listened with rapt attention. Most had never heard the story. When I finished, a brown headed boy named Ian burst into tears, jumped up, and ran away from the group.

Clueless about what had gone wrong, I went after Ian. Tenderly putting my arm around his shoulders, I inquired about his tearful response. The distraught six year old jerked out from under my arm and choked out his words through sobs; *He didn't do anything wrong! I did. He didn't deserve to die because of me!* Wow!

This six year old boy's profound emotional response to Jesus' death caused me to reevaluate my complacency. Having grown up in church, I had lost my appreciation for the magnitude of the story, and perhaps you recognize the tendency as well. The Cross is point A in the Christian life. We know the story so well that we often merely breeze through it.

The next phrase we come to though in the Love Prayer requires that we remember afresh the cross. It says, ***And I pray that you, being rooted and established in love...*** (v17). This phrase speaks of beginnings. Where does the Christian life begin but at the cross? This phrase reminds us that the sacrifice Christ made on our behalf is the irrefutable, foundational proof of God's immeasurable love for us. It is what the apostle Paul wants us to contemplate before praying for the ability to grasp God's love for us.

For that reason, I write with a strong desire to stir in you a deep response befitting such a passionate demonstration of love. To begin to understand the significance of the words *rooted and established in love,* let us begin at point A as if we were reading it for the first time:

The need for the Messiah

Roughly two thousand years ago in the scrabble-filled country of Israel, the Jews had been following God's commands to sacrifice blemish-free animals for their sins since the time of Moses. So much blood had been shed through the centuries that they knew, with certainty, that the only atonement for sin was blood. After all, they worshipped a holy God whose presence sin could not enter. The animal sacrifices of the past provided only a temporary covering for sin—a graphic picture of the seriousness of sin and the desperate need for a deliverer. God intended to fulfill His promises of a Messiah and permanently pay for man's sin through the death of his perfect, sinless Son.

The Jews knew their need and longed for the Awaited One. Every year during the Passover feast, they asked God anew to fulfill the ancient prophesies of a Messiah. Unfortunately, they expected him to come with great power and glory. Instead, the God of the Universe did the unthinkable by sending His Son as a humble servant who took on the flesh of a man and communed with a sin-cursed people. Jesus ate, drank, laughed, cried, sweat, hurt, and lived the whole gamut of human experiences; yet He did so without sin.

Just three years into a successful ministry of preaching, teaching and healing, the long-awaited Passover arrived. Jesus celebrated with his disciples and then went up to the Mount of Olives to pray. Knowing that the time had come for Him to fulfill the ancient prophesies through unimaginable suffering, Jesus fell on the ground before his Father. In such anguish of soul that He sweats great drops of blood, Jesus asked that the cup might pass from Him.

While the clueless disciples slept nearby, Jesus, in agony, prayed for them and also for all who would believe in Him. Jesus prayed; *May they be brought to complete unity to let the world know that you sent me and have loved them even as you have loved me* (**John 17:23**). What characterized Jesus' heart's desire in those moments of emotional and spiritual agony? It was that we would be unified and know God's love for us.

Suffering through multiple trials

After submitting to the Father's will, Jesus rose with renewed strength and woke His disciples to stand ready for the betrayer's arrival. How hurtful it must have been to be betrayed into enemy hands by one who had lived and followed Him during His entire ministry. The rejection, however, did not end with Judas' betrayal. With the exception of Peter and John, Jesus witnessed His closest friends flee in fear at his arrest. Then, a short time later while the temple guard struck Jesus again and again, even Peter caved into his fears and three separate times denied even knowing Jesus.

During a hastily arranged midnight trial, utterly alone Jesus faced Caiaphas the high priest and the Jewish religious leaders. Falsely accused, spit upon, and struck in the face by His own chosen people Jesus silently stood. Can you imagine the humiliation? The disgrace and abuse, though, had only just begun.

Because Roman law forbade the Jews from executing anyone, the Jewish leaders, hoping for a death sentence, sent Jesus before Pilate, the Roman governor at that time. The Jews refused to enter Pilate's palace but had the governor come out to them. This behavior stemmed from their concern over not wanting to be unclean and therefore unable to celebrate the Passover. (What a dark irony there was in the care they took to remain ceremonially clean while seeking the murder of their Messiah.) After initially resisting a role in this Jewish affair, Pilate personally questioned Jesus in search of the truth and concluded that there was no basis for the charges.

Upon learning that Jesus was a Galilean and under Herod's jurisdiction, Pilate, hoping to avoid further involvement, sent Jesus to Herod. This same cruel Herod who ordered the beheading of John the Baptist curiously wanted to see if Jesus, the famous miracle worker, might perhaps perform a miracle for him. What a spectacle! When Jesus showed no inclination to perform any supernatural displays, Herod, disappointed, turned cruel. In silence, God in the Flesh stood and endured the vicious ridicule and mockery of Herod and his soldiers. After finishing their sadistic fun, Herod returned Jesus to Pilate with no decision rendered regarding Jesus' fate.

Unimaginable suffering

Pilate, attempting to appease the Jews without the crucifixion of an innocent man, ordered that Jesus be severely flogged. Roman soldiers dished out cruelty beyond measure on our Savior during a brutal beating using various tools of their trade; the lashes eventually tore flesh from His body.

When I saw the movie The Passion of the Christ, the graphic depiction of the gruesome flogging scene when Jesus' body trembled from unimaginable pain caused a flashback of a memory of my experience in the hospital, just hours after surgery. My in-laws brought my young son to the hospital to visit me. Not wanting to be groggy or asleep during his visit, I skipped my pain medicine, little understanding the consequences of such a decision. After my son left, the pain hit me like a flood causing me to tremble uncontrollably all over. Fortunately for me, the tortuous minutes were few thanks to a nurse's quick injection of pain medicine.

With that memory etched deep in my brain, I wept for Jesus during this movie portrayal of His pain. My Savior could have stopped His suffering at any moment by the power of a word and destroyed those who dared to harm Him. Instead, out of love, He endured blow after excruciating blow. **Isaiah 53:5** says, *But he was wounded for our transgressions, he was bruised for our iniquities: the chastisement of our peace was upon him; and with his stripes we are healed* (KJV).

Unfortunately, Jesus' horrific suffering did not end after the brutal flogging. The soldiers, never weary of cruel sport, shoved a crown of thorns onto His head and placed a purple robe on His raw back. Bloody and weak, my Lord endured blows to the face and head as they mocked Him as King of the Jews.

Imagine your thoughts and emotions, had you been a silent observer in the drafty cell as that mockery and hitting took place. While watching Jesus as He silently looked at His attackers with piercingly sad eyes, occasionally clouded by the blood that dripped from His forehead, would you cry or would you rise up in angry defense of Him? Perhaps you might hide your face in shame? Whatever the response, I am quite certain that you would never be the same. Certainly, the way you lived your life would change as well. Taking His suffering for granted would be a thing of the past.

Unfortunately the worst of the Messiah's suffering still loomed before Him. Satisfied that enough had been done to satiate the rabid crowd; Pilate presented the bloodied Lord to the Jews. The mob, however, still intent on execution yelled, *Crucify him! Crucify him!* Fearing the Jews, Pilate eventually gave in and ordered Jesus' execution.

The shame and agony continued as Jesus unsuccessfully attempted to carry the heavy cross with His last remnants of strength. A stranger passing by gave aid at the Roman's insistence. Once at Golgotha, the place of crucifixion, soldiers brutally nailed Jesus' feet and hands to a wooden cross.

For years secular scholars said that the Bible gave an inaccurate description of a Roman crucifixion, stating that the Romans did not nail criminals to the cross but instead tied them. Belief in that consensus persisted until archaeologists unearthed evidence that showed how on occasion, the Romans did nail the hands and feet of particularly notorious criminals. As if it was not enough for Jesus to be beaten to the brink of death and crucified, the soldiers further tortured our Savior by nailing huge spikes through His hands and feet. Prophets prophesied that particular detail, by the way, in the Old Testament hundreds of years before the Roman Empire or crucifixion were even conceived.[24]

Producer of The Passion of the Christ, Mel Gibson, stated that audiences saw his own hands nailing the spikes into Jesus. By doing this, Mr. Gibson desired to personally acknowledge that his sins nailed Christ to the cross. The Jews and Roman soldiers did not alone perform this hideous execution. In order that the sins of every individual throughout all of time might be paid for completely, God demanded the death of Jesus Christ, the only perfect sacrifice.

Love for us sinners held Him there. The ridicule continued as Jesus hung on a cross and suffered a grueling death. At any time He could have freed himself from His torture and destroyed His crucifiers with a legion of angels. I cannot imagine the depth of love the Savior had for us in those moments of extreme suffering—unfathomable love causing Him to choose moment after agonizing moment to subject himself to what He could have ended. Thanks be to God that Jesus persevered till the task was completed! With His last breath He exclaimed, *It is finished*, and committed His spirit to the Father, dying in our place.

---

[24] Psalm 22:16 and Zachariah 12:10

Recommended viewing

If you have never watched The Passion of the Christ, I strongly urge you to do so. I know graphic gore abounds and some unnecessary additions exist. Even so, viewing the graphic portrayal of Christ's suffering proves helpful in beginning to grasp the love of God. Just try missing Christ's love for you as you watch in vivid color all that He endured to pay the penalty for your sin.

The first time I viewed it in the theater, I determined not to turn away from the portrayal of Jesus' suffering, and I literally became physically ill. The next time I watched it at home in preparation for this chapter, and this time, alone in my bedroom, I sobbed throughout the lengthy portrayal of my precious Savior's suffering. I cried as Ian did, *It's not fair Lord. You didn't deserve it! I did! You did nothing wrong.* And when it was over, I knelt by my bed and begged forgiveness for ever doubting that God loves me and thanked Him for sending His son to die in my place.

Personal decision required

Countless passages in the Bible refer to the death of Christ as the ultimate proof of His boundless love for us. *But God demonstrates His own love for us in this: While we were still sinners, Christ died for us* (**Romans 5:8**).

There is nothing that we have done to deserve such an act of love, but in His grace, He did it anyway.

If you have never trusted in Christ's death, burial, and resurrection as payment of your sin debt, I plead with you to consider that decision today. Jesus said, *I am the way and the truth and the life. No one comes to the Father except through me* (**John 14:6**). There is no other means for salvation-- not good works, church attendance, or anything else.[25] To say that you must do something, anything, to add to Christ's death is to say that His loving sacrifice on the cross proved insufficient. Choose today to take that first, huge step towards grasping the Savior's love for you by trusting Christ alone for salvation.

An analogy from gardening

Keeping the story of Jesus' death for us in mind, let us now look at the poignant meaning of the following phrase in the Love Prayer: *rooted and established in love* (v.17). Obviously a metaphor, the author likely had in mind two levels of meaning when he wrote these words. The first relates to agriculture.

Some equate gardening with sore muscles, an aching back, and a sweaty, dirty body. Others of us cannot get enough of it. We anticipate our carefully planted seed sending up tender shoots like a child anticipates Christmas

---

[25] Acts 4:12

morning. We wander our yards daily lingering over every plant as a mother does her new chicks, just to see what new flower has bloomed. The work is really just an excuse to be out breathing in the fresh air of a garden.

I spent a few years gardening before I discovered the miracle of rooting a plant. Did you know that you can turn a broken off piece of a plant into a whole new plant? Some plants root easier than others, of course, but most of them will do it if the right steps are taken. First, a piece, preferably about a foot long is cut off and stripped of all but a couple of leaves. Then, you place the almost bare stock in the soil and keep it moist for a time. Before the plant can grow it must have roots, and it may go through a time of wilting before the roots develop. New life springing out of the bare stock heralds the news that a root system has formed.

The apostle Paul uses the rooting of a plant as a picture in the Love Prayer of how we as Christians are established and rooted in love. Just as the roots of a plant form its foundation or beginning, so also do the Christian's roots. We were once dead and cut off from God, like a piece broken off from the main plant. Then, because of salvation through the grace afforded by the cross, God establishes or roots us. New life emerges from something lifeless. Christ's selfless act of love became the means for our rooting (salvation).

A root out of dry ground

Another level to this analogy must have also been on Paul's mind when he chose to use the word *rooted*. Throughout the Bible, Jesus Christ was referred to as the Root of Jesse. (Jesse was the father of King David, an ancestor of both the stepfather of Jesus—Joseph, as well as Mary-- Jesus' mother.) **Isaiah 53:2** says, He grew up *like a root out of dry ground.* In other words, the Messiah came to a barren place where nothing should have grown. Because of God's holiness, He has always hated sin. The sin-filled Earth, therefore, provided a very hostile place for God in the Flesh to spend thirty-three years. However, in this hostile environment (the dry ground), He produced branches and fruit through his death, burial, and resurrection.

Because of Jesus' love, He came and established life so that we too, though we lived in a land of death, may be rooted and established. Before Christ, we existed dead in sin, and our lives remained barren. But because of trusting in Christ's death on the cross for our sins, roots miraculously sprang from an inconceivable place for life to spring. The Root of Jesse rooted us by love.

Grasping the tremendous love of God encompasses the Love Prayer, and Paul begins it with a reminder of our point A. Here we find our loving beginning. It is only through the amazing love of God who sent His son to die for our sins that we are established into God's family. Stop now and contemplate your roots. Fathom the unfathomable.

CHAPTER 7

Just As I Am

---

*How much more, then, will the blood of Christ... **cleanse
our consciences** from acts that lead to death, so that we
may serve the living God!* (Hebrews 9:14)

Perfection – It has a nice ring to it; does it not? For
me, it became an expectation, a demand, and a relentless,
unachievable goal. How many of us strive day after day to
make ourselves good enough for God? I certainly did!
Like so many, my false view of a never satisfied God arose
from the example of well-meaning parents who placed high
demands on their children. Now, as a parent myself, it
remains a frightening and burdensome prospect knowing
that my parenting shaped my son's view of God because I
too am a fallen, imperfect sinner. Face it: Even well-
intentioned parents make mistakes in childrearing that often
misshape their children's view of God.

One small, yet indelible event from my childhood
illustrates how I came to believe that pleasing my heavenly
Father proved impossible. Like many children, I played

sports year-around. My parents faithfully attended every game, event, or race in which I competed, cheering me on with great enthusiasm. More devoted parents did not exist. Their presence was a blessing; unless that is, I did poorly.

Every summer until I turned thirteen, the local swim team filled my days with practices and meets. I loved the water and the competition. I will never forget one particular race in my tenth or eleventh year. At that meet, I swam my favorite and most competitive stroke—breaststroke. Something unknown energized me that day. At the sound of the starting gun I dove into the water, and my muscles responded with intensity. Swimming as I had never done before, I kept looking back in disbelief at the other swimmers falling farther and farther behind. I was ecstatic!

As I climbed out of the pool exhausted but jubilant over my victory, the man timing my lane announced my time. I had knocked a full twelve seconds off of my personal best and had come in first place by quite a distance. My father met me at the pool's edge, but instead of acknowledging my achievement, he said with obvious frustration; *If you had quit looking over your shoulder to see where the other swimmers were, you would have improved your time even more!* Crushed certainly described me. My best fell short, again.

False views of God

Often, people perceive God as never satisfied, judgmental and offering only conditional love. We try day after day to live the Christian life to the best of our ability. Some days we even feel successful. Then, after hearing a sermon, reading the Bible, or even just listening to those internal messages that play relentlessly in our minds we remember our failures. It would seem that we will never be good enough. We will never conquer that sin. We will never gain God's pleasure. Because we believe that God demands perfection, punishes failure, and only demonstrates a measure of love and acceptance when perfection is achieved, we grow frustrated and discouraged with the Christian life. I had a lot to learn about the real God of the Bible and needed to correct those types of half-truths. Maybe you do too.

Often a false belief that God loves conditionally couples with the view that God just waits to unleash His wrath on us if we fail. Although the Love Prayer itself does not directly address this topic, the apostle Paul spends an entire chapter leading up to the prayer that clearly and emphatically reminds Believers of God's unconditional love and complete forgiveness of sins.[26] Because this book focuses on the deep and unfailing love of Christ, I must not skip over what is a mental block for so many--God's perceived condemnation and conditional acceptance.

---

[26] Ephesians 3

The woman caught in adultery

Recently I had the privilege of listening to a sermon from a guest preacher on a passage that I have read and heard taught many times before. As I settled into my seat, confident that new insight into such a familiar Bible story proved impossible, the preacher surprised me as he drew my attention to an aspect of the story that I had never before contemplated. I want to share it with you.

Because Jesus gained ever-increasing popularity during his ministry, a group of Jewish religious leaders called the Pharisees felt threatened and looked for opportunities to discredit Him.[27] One morning in the temple, when a crowd had gathered around Jesus to hear Him teach, the Pharisees interrupted the lesson by dragging a woman caught in adultery into the gathering.

I realize that in our modern culture many of our TV shows glorify this sin, but no such cavalier attitude existed in Judea during the time of Christ. It was considered a serious breach of God's holy Law. The woman must have been terrified and humiliated beyond description. Not only was her sin being paraded in front of the town where all could click their tongues in disapproval and whisper their condemnations, but the Law of Moses demanded death by stoning for the adulterer.

As the teachers of the Law forced her to stand before Jesus, she must have hung her head in shame and

---

[27] Story taken from John 8:1-11

trembled as she saw the crowd around her picking up the ever-plentiful rocks on the ground in preparation for what would certainly come. After hushing the rumblings in the crowd, the pious Pharisees spoke up: *In the Law Moses commanded us to stone such women. Now what do you say?* (v.5).

Without responding, Jesus stooped down and began scratching words into the dirt. The perturbed leaders continued demanding an answer to their questions, but Jesus just silently continued writing. Multiple theories exist on what Jesus was writing, but the Bible remains strangely silent on that matter. We only know that after some time of this, Jesus rose and responded with a simple statement: *If any one of you is without sin, let him be the first to throw a stone at her* (v.7).

Now picture the scene: The crowd and the Pharisees surely stood around with their rocks in hand just waiting for the go- ahead. Then, after Jesus' declaration, he again stoops down and resumes his writing in the dirt. Slowly, the older men began to turn and walk away. One by one all those that just moments before anxiously awaited the opportunity to be the first to punish this woman for her egregious sin, left the scene. Perhaps they realized that they too had at some point fallen short of God's perfect standard.

Finally, when none remained save the adulterous woman, Jesus again stood and looked around at the once crowded temple area. *'Woman, where are they? Has no one condemned you?' 'No one, sir,' she said. 'Then neither do I condemn you...Go now and leave your life of sin'* (v.10-11).

Now in case you, like I, have never thought of the profound significance of a certain aspect of this story, let me share with you what the preacher pointed out that Sunday morning. This woman did indeed deserve judgment and condemnation for her failure to keep the perfect Law of God. Likely, all around her people held stones ready to condemn her to death. However, Jesus, the one who created the Law given to Moses, and therefore the one who had the ultimate right to condemn her, held no stone. Did you catch that? Jesus held no stone! He wanted to bring her to repentance not condemn her, as evidenced by His final statement for her to leave her life of sin.

Jesus met God's standard of perfection for us

Dear Christian, is there a sin or failure in your past or present that is preventing you from walking in the love of your Savior? Remember the words in **1John 2:1&2: *But if anybody does sin, we have one who speaks to the Father in our defense—Jesus Christ, the Righteous One. He is the atoning sacrifice for our sins...*** Yes, God does demand perfection! This is indeed a fact of the holy nature of The Almighty. He knew; however, that we could never achieve perfection and so took action on our behalf.

Because of what Christ did at the cross, God transferred the righteousness of Christ to us the moment we put our trust in Jesus. *Through the obedience of one man the many will be made righteous.*[28]

Take a moment now to picture the Lord, with no stone in hand but tremendous love in His eyes, telling you simply to leave your sin and failures behind. Let it go. The Bible states emphatically that there is *no condemnation for those who are in Christ Jesus,* and *I will forgive their wickedness and remember their sins no more.*[29]

The Bible does indeed portray a God of wrath because He is holy and that holiness does indeed demand payment for sin—justice. As a result we must never take our sin lightly as a mere frivolous occurrence. *Shall we go on sinning so that grace may increase? By no means!* [30] However, the entire Old Testament reveals God's beautiful, overarching plan that prepared a way for His eternal wrath to be completely satisfied. That plan allows us to stand in His presence, spotless and free from condemnation because of Christ.

Is the cross sufficient for your failures?

Holding on to self-punishment, guilt, and shame after confessing your sin is like saying that Christ's death

---

[28] Romans 5:19b
[29] Romans 8:1 & Hebrews 8:12
[30] Romans 6:1

on the cross proves insufficient for your sin. Do you really believe that? Make a conscious choice right now to let go of the self-condemnation, thereby freeing you to accept the Father's incredible love for you.

Just today God brought to my mind an egregious sin of my past. I had previously confessed this sin but never really saw the seriousness of it, and therefore, had not truly repented. As I sat in my recliner by the window with God's Word in my lap, I began to review some verses that I had memorized the day before. While quoting those verses, God opened my eyes to something I had previously overlooked. Through that fresh insight, He impressed upon me His perspective of my sin and just how seriously He viewed it. Suddenly, the Holy Spirit overwhelmed me with the shame and guilt of having grieved my precious Lord.

I initially reacted by wanting to punish myself by wallowing for a time in the shame I felt. After all, surely I deserved it for failing my Savior. But, because I had beside me all of the verses on forgiveness and sin, written down in preparation for this chapter, I began to read over them. Verse after verse reminded me of the truth. Yes, I had sinned. Yes, I had failed to meet God's perfect standard, but Jesus already paid for that sin. **Proverbs 28:13** reminded me that *he who conceals his sins does not prosper, but whoever confesses and renounces them finds mercy.*

I confessed my sin to the Lord and made a commitment to turn from that sin. As a result, God immediately freed me to accept His mercy and again commune with Him. As I read over the words of **Psalm 32:1**, I found the final assurance I needed. *Blessed is he whose transgressions are forgiven, whose sins are covered. Blessed is the man whose sin the Lord does not count against him and in whose spirit is no deceit.* I was blessed (which means happy) not condemned, and you can be too! The blood of Christ remains sufficient!

The story behind "Just as I Am"

Like many from my generation and before who grew up in the church, I learned the great hymns of the Faith. Although I did not fully appreciate what I perceived to be antiquated at the time, as an adult the depth of those praises and expressions of biblical truths is now a rich heritage. Many of the hymn writers penned their songs out of personal suffering and therefore great understanding of God's love and mercy. One such hymn writer was Charlotte Elliot.

Miss Elliot was born in Clapham, England in 1789 to a family with a godly heritage. As a young woman she became known for her satirical writing and cartoons, but at the age of thirty began to suffer from a degenerative disease that left her irritable due to constant pain.

Many also said she had the voice of an angel. In spite of her illness, in 1834 she took the opportunity to debut at a London concert, which a notable pastor, Dr. Malan, attended. Upon hearing her sing, he felt compelled to speak to Charlotte of her need for Christ, and how her great talent could be used for God's glory. Without concern for decorum, this man of God addressed Miss Elliott during the dinner that followed the concert. Indignantly, she replied that she did not wish to discuss it, stomped her feet, and rudely turned to walk away. Upon seeing her response, Dr. Malan called out apologetically, *I did not mean to offend you. But I want you to know that Jesus can save you if you will turn to Him.*

For days she wrestled with God over her need for Him. She knew her rudeness and irritableness were wrong. Then, three weeks after the concert, her family went to a dinner that Dr. Malan also attended in the home of some friends. She confessed to him how his previous words had stirred her heart and asked him how she might be saved. He told her, *Just come to him as you are*, and she did.

Her salvation may have saved her soul and given her much joy, but it did not free her body from a prison of pain.   Her parents and siblings all actively involved themselves in ministry in their churches and community, but Charlotte frequently found herself unable to join them due to her condition.   On one such occasion, she stayed home alone while her family helped her brother, who was a pastor, raise money for a school for the children of poor clergymen.

Rather then give way to the depression that lurked in her mind, she determined to write a hymn that might be sold to raise money for the school. Acutely aware of her own failings, the words of Dr. Malan, which had dramatically changed her life fourteen years previously, came to mind. His words became the foundation of her hymn, which God used to raise more money for the school than all of the other family fundraisers combined, as well as to minister to countless people through the ages. Charlotte titled the hymn, *Just as I Am*.

The first two stanzas highlight the Gospel very simply and poetically, but more than that, they remind us of the point of this chapter—that God takes us just as we are, imperfect sinners.

Just as I am, without one plea,
But that Thy blood was shed for me,
And that Thou bidst me come to Thee,
O Lamb of God, I come, I come.

Just as I am, and waiting not
To rid my soul of one dark blot,
To Thee whose blood can cleanse each spot,
O Lamb of God, I come, I come.

The next stanza highlights the inward struggle that Charlotte knew profoundly, as do many of us.

Just as I am, though tossed about
With many a conflict, many a doubt,

Fightings and fears within, without,
O Lamb of God, I come, I come.

Lastly, as you read the remaining stanzas, take notice of the solution she describes to our inward conflict, and determine today to come to the Lord of love just as you are.

Just as I am, Thou wilt receive,
Wilt welcome, pardon, cleanse, relieve;
Because Thy promise I believe,
O Lamb of God, I come, I come.

Just as I am, Thy love unknown
Hath broken every barrier down;
Now, to be Thine, yea, Thine alone,
O Lamb of God, I come, I come.

Just as I am, of that free love
The breadth, length, depth, and height to prove,
Here for a season, then above,
O Lamb of God, I come, I come!

CHAPTER 8

The Necessity of the Body

And I pray that you, being rooted and established in love,
*may have power, **together with all the saints,***
to grasp how wide and long and high and deep
is the love of Christ (Ephesians 3:17b-18)

Life crept discouragingly by, while day after day, I lay in bed extremely ill. Once again my Sunday worship took place in bed, alone. Meanwhile, a dear women attending church that day asked my husband how I fared. After learning of my condition, she called me to determine how she might help. Although too sick to speak at the time, she persisted and called back the following day. Even though I resisted Mary Anne's attempts at discovering how she could assist me, she showed up at my door later that day with groceries, dinner for my family, loving encouragement for me, and a ride for my son to a play practice he had that evening. Obviously, God demonstrated

His love for me during my suffering through this saint's kindness. What an example that portrays of the way God designed His church to function! It also provides a fine example of why Paul interjects a seemingly out-of-place phrase at this point in the Love Prayer.

Clearly the apostle intended the Love Prayer for individuals. Yet, it momentarily turns to a corporate prayer with the use of one simple phrase: *together with all the saints.* I bet that when you initially read through this prayer, you did what is so easy to do--to skip right over this phrase, never realizing the significance of those five words. By adding them, Paul makes a crucial point. He wants the church as a whole, not just the individual believer, to have the power to grasp the love of Christ. Furthermore, and this is crucial; God best demonstrates His love through *all the saints.*

Who are the saints?

Many think that a saint is an individual who has done great works for the Lord in history and whom the Catholic Church has chosen to grant sainthood. Scripture certainly says otherwise. People concocted the aforementioned idea, not God. Instead, the Bible refers to all believers as saints. The New Testament alone uses the word *saint* roughly sixty times in reference to any believer in Christ. The Greek word means, *sacred, (physically pure, blameless or religious, ceremonially consecrated) -- most holy*[31] (Many translations now substitute the word *saint* with a something else like *holy people*, but the Greek word has not changed.) What a joke! Most Christians often stray from purity, blamelessness, or holiness: Right? However, when God looks at someone who has placed his faith in Christ's shed blood as payment for that individual's sin, only the righteousness or purity of Christ remains. The last part of 1 **John 1:7** says, *And the blood of Jesus, his Son, purifies us from all sin.* In other words, people do not become saints through their own faulty efforts; instead, they are **declared** holy or blameless because of the righteousness of Christ. Therefore, all believers are indeed saints.

The Body of Christ

Analogies fill the Bible to help us understand spiritual truths by comparing those truths to familiar things. The New Testament writers use the human body and its many varying parts as an analogy of the church.[32] We have one physical body that consists of many parts (arms, legs, brain, etc.), each of which serves a unique purpose.

Recently my son had a cold. It was nothing major, but as we sat at the table to eat a delicious dinner, I noticed

---

[31] Strong's Exhaustive Concordance of the Bible #40
[32] Romans 12:4-5

that he looked miserable as his mouth hung open, gasping for air between bites. His stopped up nose made it quite difficult to breathe and eat at the same time. After I sympathetically commented on his apparent misery, he replied that, worse yet, he could not even taste what he knew must be yummy. (It is great how kids love their mom's cooking!) Suddenly, my son recognized the value of the seemingly insignificant nose when it temporarily failed to perform its normal duties.

Just as my son discovered with his cold, each part of the body, no matter how small, is necessary and important to the ideal functioning of the entire body. Likewise, **1 Corinthians 12:27** makes this clear when it says, *Now you are the body of Christ, and each one of you is a part of it.* A church has many members or parts, and God designed each one to serve a unique purpose. This design adds value and aids in the proper functioning of the church as a whole.

God's hands of love

In addition to using our gifts to benefit the Body, the number one characteristic of absolutely every Christian should be loving behavior. This defining love should be demonstrated within the church body. A predominant theme of **1 John** is that because God loves us, we should also love others— specifically those within the Body.

Chapter **4:11-12** says, *Dear friends, since God so loved us, we also ought to love one another. No one has ever seen God; but if we love each other, God lives in us and his love is made complete in us.* Let me paraphrase for emphasis: We cannot see God who loves us, so He designed the church to be His hands of love in others' lives. For the proper functioning of the Body, each individual needs to participate. The body needs your gifts but also your demonstration of love towards others. That is God's perfect design for the church. Of course, that design demands active involvement by each member of the church, not merely pew-warming for an hour or two a week. Can you be a Mary Anne?

This perfect design for the church creates a problem for some. Bitter toward God and fearful of being a part of His church, several people whom I have encountered through the years find active or even passive involvement with His Body difficult. Negative experiences with churches abound. I am convinced that some of these incidences come from unbelievers within churches. Still other hurtful incidences occur simply because believers are forgiven, not perfect. Either way, the results often prove devastating, and I know it must grieve God.

In contrast, I have also witnessed countless instances where the church worked beautifully together to be God's hands of goodness, love, and strength in the lives of people. Throughout the years of my life I have personally experienced this on many occasions, in several different churches, and in three different states. I have also had the opportunity to be a part of ministering to many others within the Body.

The Smith's story

Take, for example, the way my church ministered to one family as they went through a great trial. This couple, whom I will call John and Kathy Smith, had only been attending a short while when their ordeal began. Without explanation, the Smith's only child, a nine year old boy, became listless, started losing weight and having frequent diarrhea. Their doctor seemed infuriatingly unconcerned and scheduled them for an appointment with a gastroenterologist a month out. You can imagine the fears that consumed the Smith's every thought. Out of her distress, Kathy began regularly updating our church via e-mail. She wrote honestly of her fears, panic attacks, and struggles in handling the current crisis.

The church responded beautifully. Church members reached out to them in a variety of ways. People, some they knew and some they did not, began calling just to pray with them. Someone Kathy had never even met before came and cleaned her house. Because she was too preoccupied to cook, we brought her meals or just came to sit with Kathy to prevent her from feeling so alone.

As their son continued to lose weight at an alarming rate, Kathy pursued the overwhelming task of researching nutritional treatment options for whatever might possibly be the problem. On one particular trip to a health food store, she asked for help from a clerk. While discussing her son's symptoms with this stranger, Kathy broke down in tears. To her surprise, the sympathetic clerk was a believer. While standing in the store aisle, the clerk prayed for the Smith's situation. Even in something as small but trying as a trip to the store, God used one of His people to let Kathy know that she was not alone.

When the doctors finally diagnosed the Smith's son with Crohn's Disease and admitted him to the hospital for treatment, the church members put together an enormously huge gift basket and took it to their son. Despite the trial's continuation and the despair that could have come with such a diagnosis, Kathy's e-mails changed. They began to be filled with praise and thanks to God for the comfort and encouragement His people brought to their family during their time of need. The entire family could see and feel God's hands of love in a very real way through His people.

That example is not just an isolated and remarkable instance of the church functioning the way God intended for it to function. Quite literally, I could fill a book with story after story of instances such as those.

When God established the church at Pentecost, He did so for multiple reasons. Yes, the spread of the Gospel tops the list. God also intended to form a ministering body of love on this earth. God purposed for *the whole body, joined and held together by every supporting ligament, (to) grow and build itself up in love, as each part does its work* (**Ephesians 4:15-16**). Functioning according to God's plan, the church has a tremendously positive impact on people's lives, just like in the story of the Smiths.

Actions speak loudly

Have you ever been hurting; I mean really hurting, and God's Word and other's remarks, kind and true as they might be seemed hollow? I certainly have. When I was falsely accused of child abuse, I heard and received notes with the typical, Christian platitudes, from well-meaning people wanting to encourage me. Sadly though, after my son was taken away, I was terribly angry at God. I quit reading his Word and was, therefore, no longer open to God's words of love and comfort for me. Underneath my spiritual façade, I silently argued away Christians' words or simply dismissed what they expressed all together. Their words may have been true, but my hurting heart rendered them meaningless. To my surprise though, God had plenty of nonverbal means for communicating His love as the *hands* of His body reached out to our family.

For example, when a family stocked our refrigerator and cabinets with food, my arguments fell silent. When our church helped pay for our car to be fixed so that we would have a means of transportation to leave the state, I cried tears of humble gratitude. When Christians took us into their homes to provide a safe place to live so that our son might be safe from the state while we prepared a legal defense, I felt cared for. When about thirty people from our church showed up at the courthouse at 8:30 A.M., for what was supposed to be a one hour hearing to determine the fate of our family, and then stayed in the lobby even though the hearing continued off and on until 7 P.M., just to be with us during our darkest hours, I felt awe. When hundreds of Christians who knew us from several different states, tied up the judge's fax line for days in order to write in support of our innocence, I felt encouraged in spite of the judge's annoyed response. When a Christian family we knew and trusted volunteered to be foster parents, and then lovingly cared for our son for over three weeks, I felt grateful beyond expression. When a Christian woman who had never met me or my son sent him small care packages and notes of encouragement, almost daily while he lived in foster care, I felt comforted. When a Christian attorney donated his services to represent our son separately from our representation, I felt pleasantly shocked. When Christians made financial sacrifices to donate to our overwhelming expenses, I became speechless. When Christians made a trip to Disney and the local go-cart track possible to provide fun distractions for our son whose life was in upheaval, we found laughter and pleasure in the midst of great heartache. The list goes on and on, but you get the idea.[33]

Arguing with God's Word and ranting at my Creator over His apparent lack of love for me and my family came naturally from such painful circumstances. However, I could not argue away or deny the demonstrations of His love that His Body showed me in His name. My church lived out John's words in **1 John 3:18** when he said, ***Dear children, let us not love with words or tongue but with actions and in truth.*** Eventually, those loving actions broke through to my hurting and angry heart and changed my perspective of God's love in my time of crisis.

What if our family had not been obedient to **Hebrews 10:25** when the crisis came, which says, ***not giving up meeting together, as some are in the habit of doing, but encouraging one another—and all the more as you see the Day approaching***? We would have cut off God's primary tool for showing His tremendous love towards myself and my family when our need was the greatest.

Tying it all together

---

[33] To hear an audio recording of the complete story of this time in our family, go to www.heartandminidministries.com. "The Julin Story--A Struggle with Man & God."

Now, let's get back to the phrase in the Love Prayer, *together with all the saints.* Why does Paul include this seemingly insignificant phrase right before he makes the request to grasp the love of Christ? Paul does so because it is primarily through the collective involvement of the saints that an individual has the opportunity to experience the love of God. Why? Because, God designed the church to be His on-going earthly hands of love.

If you are not actively participating in a local Body of Christ, then you have cut off God's chosen instrument of love in your life. Likewise, you limit your ability to be obedient to God by showing His love to other saints. You may, therefore, never comprehend the love of Christ that continues day after day, regardless of our behavior or circumstances.

If you are one of those people I referred to earlier who has had bad experiences with the church, I know that the prospect of finding and getting involved in a church proves daunting. However, throughout the world a multitude of Bible-teaching, loving churches do exist. I understand how difficult it can be to make that step, but it truly is necessary. The Bible speaks clearly on this.

Tell God your concerns and fears about finding a good church. He cares and will lead you. I implore you to do some research, ask around, and then start visiting. If the church you visit lacks friendliness, and/or they are not teaching God's Word faithfully, try another one. Upon finding one you feel good about, you must get involved. You will be blessed!

If you are currently attending a good church but are merely putting in your one or two hours a week pew-warming, start praying and looking for ways that you can become a functioning part of the Body of Christ. God's perfect plan includes everyone in the church, not just a select few.

The one-time demonstration of God's love through Christ at the cross rooted and established us. After a plant forms roots, though, it requires ongoing nurturing to grow. Similarly, the depths of God's love continue to manifest itself as we grow in the faith through the working of the body of believers. This occurs when *each part does its work.*

CHAPTER 9

The Limitless
Love of Christ for You

may have power, together with all the saints, **to grasp**
how wide and long and high and deep is the
love of Christ, (Ephesians 3:18b-19)

Although I practice and advocate having daily meal times together, gathered around a table as a family, once a week our family had a *special night*. On these nights we could be found eating dinner on TV trays while watching a movie. Although once cherished by my son, my husband and I viewed the event in a slightly different light. We enjoyed seeing him happy and hearing him laugh. You see; the endless amusement he had for silly humor and childlike plots gave us one more way to practice selflessness as we consented to his viewing choices. Oh, what sacrifices parents often make for their little darlings!

Thankfully, our son's interests also included a love for nature and occasionally the chosen movie reflected that interest. One *special night* we watched a documentary called <u>Deep Blue</u>. It revealed breathtaking footage of the ocean and its inhabitants, some of which had never before been caught on tape. Footage of the frozen oceans of the poles, the tropic waters of the equator, the various shorelines of the continents, and the very depths of the sea filled the screen. My son and I, being the more expressive members of our family, *Oohed* and *ahhed* unabashedly at the wonders of God's incredible creation.

The most awe-inspiring part of the DVD comes when special submarines take divers to the deepest reaches of the ocean ever seen by man. Dwarfing the Grand Canyon, the Marianas Trench cuts a path across the ocean's floor, plummeting as deep as eight miles below the water's surface. At these depths total darkness presides. Glacial chill and colossal pressure seem to make life in such a place impossible, and yet an incredible array of sea creatures thrives. Even there God demonstrates His handiwork.

Many of the creatures of the abyss create bioluminescent light in a brightly colored spectrum. Picture a laser show in pitch blackness and you have the general idea. To mislead its predators, one particular shrimp-like creature shoots out flares of radiantly purple light. Another creature appears as a halo of constantly changing colored light as it glides through the deep. Fewer people have traveled to those remote depths than have traveled into outer space. Precious little is known about the life inhabiting those depths, but the very existence of creative life there speaks of God's far-reaching presence. A glimpse into the seemingly infinite dimensions of creation helps to illustrate the next section of the Love Prayer. Picking up where we left off, Paul continues with a plea for us to be able *to grasp how wide and long and high and deep is the love of Christ.* When those words are considered in light of the dimensions of our world and its universe, one gets a taste of the magnitude of the love of Christ.

The scope of the universe

On a trip to a science museum, I noticed a series of large pictures displayed on a wall of many of the galaxies in our universe. Each galaxy is unique and immense. Our own Milky Way Galaxy, due to its phenomenal size, will never be seen by humans from the outside. It boggles the mind to try to grasp the size of the farthest known reaches of the universe, to say nothing of the unknown reaches. Even in our limited knowledge of space we have an indication of God's awesome handiwork. For example, did you know that the Vox Galaxy has a black hole that forms a perfect picture of the cross?

At the time Paul wrote the Love Prayer, people knew little or nothing concerning the extent of the universe or the depths of the ocean floor. However, the apostle knew from Old Testament Scripture that God's presence extended farther than mans' eyes could see. Perhaps he thought of this passage in **Job 11:7- 9**.

Can you search out the deep things of God? Can you find out the limits of the Almighty?

They are higher than heaven-- what can you do? Deeper than Sheol-- what can you know?

Their measure is longer than the earth and broader than the sea (NKJ).

Why does Paul enumerate the four dimensions of the love of Christ in the Love Prayer just like the author of Job did? Why not simply pray that we might grasp God's love? Is he merely being poetic or is he making a specific point? In order to answer those questions, let us consider the nature of the Creator.

The character of God

Can a dog be anything other than a dog? Can a fish decide to breathe air? Of course not! The character of all creatures dictates their behavior. Similarly, God's character dictates His behavior. His holy character dictates that He cannot sin or tolerate sin. His justice dictates that He must do right with regard to the righteous and the unrighteous. **1 John 4:16** says, *God is love*. God and the loving aspect of His character are one. Therefore, when the biblical writers itemize the dimensions of Almighty God, they also itemize the dimensions of His ever consistent loving character. In other words, if God's presence goes deeper than Hell, higher than Heaven, longer than our earth and wider than our seas, then His love does as well. God cannot be separate from who He is—His character.

In similar fashion to the passage in Job, King David describes in **Psalm 139:7-12** another attribute of God's character—His omnipresence. David, however, places emphasis on the comfort it brings to know God's limitless presence.

> *Where can I go from Your Spirit? Or where can I flee from Your presence? If I ascend into heaven, You are there; if I make my bed in hell, behold, You are there.*

> *If I take the wings of the morning, and dwell in the uttermost parts of the sea, even there Your hand shall lead me, and Your right hand shall hold me.*

> *If I say, Surely the darkness shall fall on me, even the night shall be light about me; Indeed, the darkness shall not hide from You, but the night*

shines as the day; the darkness and the light are both alike to You (NKJ).

In the Love Prayer, Paul mimics Old Testament writers by enumerating the unending dimensions of Christ's love for a purpose--to emphasize the far reaching, limitless nature of Christ's love. Picture the vastness of our oceans. His love for you is wider. Visualize the length of our beautiful planet Earth. His love for you is longer. Imagine the height of the seemingly unending heavens. His love for you is higher. Plummet to the deepest reaches of hell. Yes, His love for you goes deeper. You cannot escape the love of Christ because it has no boundaries. Rest in that amazing truth!

Christ's unfailing love

Furthermore, the Scripture tells us that Jesus, God's own Son, existed from the beginning with His Father.[34] The triune God has always existed and has no end.[35] He defines time, not the other way around.

So it makes perfect sense when Scripture tells us that God's love never fails. **Psalm 143:8** says, *Let the morning bring me word of your unfailing love, for I have put my trust in you.* Also, **Psalm 33:5** says, *The Lord*

---

[34] John 1:1-3
[35] Revelation 21:6

loves righteousness and justice; the earth is full of his unfailing love. We can fully trust in our Lord because His love never fails. It is not bound by time or place. The triune God has no limits and therefore either does His love. Do you long to believe that this God of love truly loves you in particular--unconditionally and unfailingly? I know I did. I desperately needed a way to break free of my misconceptions about God and His love and maybe you do as well.

A challenge

The first step in beginning to perceive God's love for me personally occurred when I accepted my counselor's challenge. I now pass that challenge on to you: Determine right now to make a conscious decision to begin trusting all of God's Word as true in your life. Yes, that means trusting it when it says God loves you; even when you do not understand it or feel the truth of it.

For over thirty years I have been a Christian, following God with all my heart. Tragically, I never really sensed, until recently, that He truly loves me. I attempted to please Him in order to gain His love. Such an approach only left me feeling woefully inadequate and desperately hurt, especially when it seemed God only responded by dishing out more pain. I tried ceaselessly to secure a sense of His love, but my efforts proved as successful as trying to hold on to a morning mist as the sun rises. Despair filled many of my days. How could I give so much of myself and yet feel so unloved?

A dramatic change

When I began meditating, studying, and praying the Love Prayer, I did so with an intense desire to understand its words. I felt compelled to begin writing this book after subtle changes began to occur in my thinking, even though I still did not grasp His love. It seemed as though I stood on the outside of a door long closed to me that had now opened just enough to see a glimpse of something wonderful. I prayed the words of the prayer with a sense of urgency for weeks, believing that they must be true for me but still lacking understanding.

My thinking on God's love towards me could best be described as a page with two columns on it. Column One—*Pain and Suffering*. Column Two—*Evidence of God's Love*. Oh, how long the list in column one extended and yet only, *Christ's death on the cross* appeared in column two. Now granted, Christ's death and the salvation it brought are beyond huge, but what evidence existed of God's love towards me after the cross?

Then something simple but dramatic changed. God revealed to me that I blamed Him for the horrible events related to the false accusation of child abuse that resulted in my son being taken away. Rather than putting the responsibility in the lap of the evil people involved, where it belonged, I held God responsible. This hurt and anger towards God clouded my ability to accurately interpret *Column One*. Pain blinded me.

When I stopped blaming God, a wonderful transformation occurred in my perspective. God opened my eyes to see how He had lovingly provided, sustained, cared for, strengthened and watched over my family and me during our darkest hours. I no longer stand mystified regarding His apparent vendetta against me. There was no vendetta! He has lovingly worked on my behalf for years.

Free will allows for the possibility of evil

I understand why many people blame God for all kinds of painful things. After all, He is all-powerful. Almighty God could prevent evil, pain, and suffering if He chose. When God created man, however, He desired to love and be loved by that creation. Love must include free will. By allowing man to have a choice (free will), the opportunity for evil (sin) entered the world.

Unfortunately, in a sin-cursed world full of sinful people who make sinful choices, many frequently get hurt. Like in the cases of a sexual abuse or murder, much suffering comes at the hands of people exercising their free-will.

Often though, the pain that people blame God for results from their own personal decisions to do things contrary to God's way. ***Proverbs 19:3*** speaks of this when it says, ***A person's own folly leads to their ruin, yet their heart rages against the Lord.*** For example, a mother chooses to drink while pregnant and then blames God for allowing her child to become deformed in the womb. Then, the child grows up to blame God for a condition caused by his mother. Or, a man who chooses to drive recklessly in the rain blames God because he ends up in an accident that leaves him with physical pain for years to come. Then, his wife blames God for their financial condition when her husband can no longer work.

Sadly, the number of scenarios like those seems endless. Ask yourself if any of what you blame God for falls into this category. After placing the responsibility on those to whom it belongs, be freed of that anger by asking God for help as you seek to forgive yourself or those who have harmed you.

God does not take away your free will or anyone else's in order to prevent pain. However, He does demonstrate His love in the midst of your pain by being your Rock in the storm, your provider in times of need, your sustainer when hope seems nonexistent, your comforter in grief, your tower of strength in weakness, and most importantly—the One who brings good into your life and the lives of others through your pain.

God brings good out of evil

Nowhere in Scripture can we see more clearly God's redemption of evil circumstances into good than in the story of Joseph from the book of Genesis. After his own brothers sold the teenage Joseph into Egyptian slavery, his master's wife falsely accused him of sexually assaulting her. Joseph lived righteously, and yet God allowed him to be put in prison for a crime he did not commit. To top it all off, he remained in prison until he was thirty years old![36]

God could have prevented his brothers and slave owners from making evil choices that negatively affected the innocent and righteous Joseph, but He did not. In God's foreknowledge, He orchestrated the events of Joseph's life for a greater purpose. Yet, in the midst of his slavery the Bible says; *The Lord was with Joseph and he prospered*[37] and again when Joseph was put in prison; *the Lord was with him; he showed him kindness and granted him favor in the eyes of the prison warden.*[38] God knew the difficult events that must transpire to bring about the salvation of two nations, but He did not abandon Joseph for a moment.

In addition to God's blessings throughout thirteen years of great hardship, Almighty God brought further redemption by raising Joseph up to be the second highest

---

[36] Genesis 41:46
[37] Genesis 39:2
[38] Genesis 39:21

ruler in the land of Egypt. That position enabled him to carry out God's plan to save the Egyptians and the Jews from starvation during seven years of famine. Many thousands were saved. Joseph also personally recognized God's loving work on his behalf. When one of Joseph's sons was born, he named the child Ephraim and said, *It is because God has made me fruitful in the land of my suffering.*[39]

For a good deal of his life, it seems that Joseph had every right to hate God and his brothers for what had happened to him. At the peak of Joseph's power, he controlled the fate of others by granting or denying food during the years of famine. To Joseph's surprise the instruments of his suffering stood before him, and he was given the perfect opportunity for revenge. His brothers had arrived in Egypt hoping to secure provisions to take back to Judea.

Upon the revelation of Joseph's identity, his brothers fell down trembling before him. They knew they deserved his wrath. Their lives were in his hands. Joseph, however, out of a changed perspective on the painful events of his life, gave a stunning reply to his brothers' request for mercy and forgiveness. *But as for you*, he says, *You meant evil against me; but God meant it for good, in order to bring it about as it is this day, to save many people alive* (Genesis 50:20 NKJ).

---

[39] Genesis 41:52

Every good gift is from God

People like me can quickly blame God for anything bad that comes their way but slowly recognize the good that comes from Him. **James 1:16-17** says, *Do not be deceived my dear brothers. Every good and perfect gift is from above, coming down from the Father of the heavenly lights, who does not change like shifting shadows.* Every good thing comes from God, and yet, often we respond to those gifts with indifference, as though we earned or deserved them. Blinded by misdirected anger and hurt, we easily fail to recognize the significant gifts God, in His love, showers daily on us.

God warns the Israelites in the book of Deuteronomy to recognize and remember God's many gifts to them.

When the LORD your God brings you into the land he swore to your fathers, to Abraham, Isaac and Jacob, to give you-- a land with large, flourishing cities you did not build, houses filled with all kinds of good things you did not provide, wells you did not dig, and vineyards and olive groves you did not plant-- then when you eat and are satisfied, be careful that you do not forget the LORD, who brought you out of Egypt, out of the land of slavery (**Deuteronomy 6:10-12**).

In other words, God wants us to take notice of every good thing in our lives. He gave them all! Each one shows His love for us. On different occasions, I have learned the lesson of taking notice of God's daily gifts the hard way. For two years, I pleaded with God to give me another child, blaming God and growing angry with Him when my prayer continually went unanswered. Then, God used my precious son being taken away to open my eyes. So blinded by discontent, I had failed to fully appreciate the blessing of the one son I already had--God's incredible gift.

We all take so many physical things for granted as if the ability to breathe, see, hear, feel touch, and move are unalienable rights. I learned this lesson the hard way. I had always taken for granted the freedom of movement from healthy legs. It had never occurred to me that a functioning body part was a gift from my heavenly Father, until I woke up one night, tried to get out of bed, and could not walk. The ability to walk normally eventually returned, and now, I consider each day that my legs work properly to be another gift from God that shows His love for me.

Later my health deteriorated significantly again and my strength disappeared. The few steps from the bed to the bathroom exhausted me. A stool supported me while I brushed my teeth or took a shower. Fear that this weakness was permanent consumed me and brought despair. When God later healed me completely (a thrilling story for another time[40]), I looked at walking and running with different eyes. What a gift of love from God physical strength truly is! I began a lasting daily habit of walking and running with the Lord. Most runners run with goals in mind like competition. I run because I literally feel God's love with each step and so praise and prayer come easily.

Ongoing proof of God's love

While searching the Bible for examples of God's love (other than the gift of His Son), Psalm 136 came to mind. The repetition of the sentence, **His love endures forever**, occurs in all twenty-six verses of this Psalm. This repetition follows twenty-six specific instances of God's good gifts to the Israelites throughout their history, giving proof of His ongoing love for them. (I urge you to read Psalm 136, even though I am not including it in the book.)

After rereading this Psalm, I decided that I needed to write a psalm following that model to force myself to ponder God's good gifts to me throughout my life. I will share a part of that writing here in hopes that you will take the idea and do it for yourself. It is a powerful exercise, which may forever change your perspective on God's ongoing love in your life.

---

[40] To hear an audio recording of the story of how God healed me, go to www.heartandmindministries.com to the speaking tab--full audio lessons and select, "A Heart at Peace."

To Him who knew me before I was born,
His love endures forever.
and put me in a family where I would hear the
Gospel,
His love endures forever.
and saved me as a child of six.
His love endures forever.
Who provided the money and the means
His love endures forever.
to travel & serve Him around the world as a teen.
His love endures forever.
To Him who gave me supportive parents
His love endures forever.
who were there cheering me on in everything I did.
His love endures forever.
To Him who gave me arms, legs, & a brain that
work
His love endures forever.
so that I might do and have many experiences.
His love endures forever.
To Him who led me to my wonderful husband
His love endures forever.
and over twenty years of blessed marriage.
His love endures forever.
To Him who has provided financially for us
His love endures forever.
when we couldn't make it on our own.
His love endures forever.

To Him who blessed me with godly in-laws
His love endures forever.
who have showered me with unconditional love.
His love endures forever.
Who allowed my body once to conceive
His love endures forever.
and brought forth my precious son.
His love endures forever.
To Him who freed us from our enemies
His love endures forever.
and brought my son safely home again.
His love endures forever.
To Him who gave me His priceless Word,
His love endures forever.
so that I might know Him and His love for me.
His love endures forever.
To Him who created such a beautiful world
His love endures forever.
and gave me eyes to see that amazing creation.
His love endures forever.
To Him who provided a nice place to call home
His love endures forever.
and a yard in which to garden.
His love endures forever.
To Him who is preparing an eternal home for me
His love endures forever.
where I can be with him
His love endures forever.

and never again be sick, sad, or in pain.
His love endures forever.
"Give thanks to the God of heaven.
His love endures forever"
(adapted from Psalm 136).

Hopefully the repetition emphasizes my point: We must gain an accurate picture of our lives so that we cannot possibly miss the evidence of God's love for us. Pain and suffering will always be a part of life on this sin-cursed earth, but God still abundantly showers us with His love.

God desires that all His children see past the pain of this life and into His love. Such a transformation truly does require some of that miraculous power for which the Love Prayer requests. For the first time in my life, I believe and feel the truth of the words of the prophet Jeremiah when he said; *I have loved you with an everlasting love; I have drawn you with loving kindness* (**Jer. 31:3**). What an incredible feeling that is!

As you read my words, does your soul cry from deep within, *I want to grasp His love too, but I don't know how.* In tears, I spoke those very words to my counselor, and God led me to the Love Prayer. God WANTS us *to grasp how wide and long and high and deep is the love of Christ.* His love for you is ongoing. His love for you is unfailing. His love for you is unconditional. His love for you is limitless. Allow God, through His miraculous power, to change your perspective of your life so that you too can grasp the dimensions of His love. Take the struggle to Christ who can open your eyes and make the truth a part of you. Keep praying!

CHAPTER 10

Grasping & Knowing Christ's Love for You

*to **grasp** how wide and long and high and deep is the love of Christ, **and to know this love that surpasses knowledge*** (Ephesians 3:18b-19)

It would be an understatement to say that our dog, Cerberus, loved to play with a tennis ball. In fact, he almost always greeted us with his little tail wagging and a ball in his mouth. However, in his enthusiasm he could not bring himself to let go of the ball long enough for us to play fetch with him. When we did succeed in getting the ball away from him, we had to throw it quickly because he immediately tried every possible means to recover it. When it was held up high, his little Jack Russell Terrier legs propelled him upward, again and again, in an attempt to get it back. What an adorable sight this made! If we hid it from him, he frantically searched every conceivable hiding spot. Once he even managed to jump on top of his doghouse to recover the ball from what my son thought was the perfect hiding place. And, of course, when we threw the ball, he eagerly raced after it.

By picturing the dog's behavior toward the ball, you can understand the Greek meaning of the word *grasp*, which means, *to take eagerly, i.e. seize, possess, comprehend, etc. literally or figuratively*[41] Paul used this verb to describe the action he wants us to be empowered to take in comprehending the limitless love of Christ. He desired that we would eagerly seize or possess an understanding of God's love for ourselves.

A down day

I will be honest with you. Today I am struggling. Money has been tight the last couple of months. One unexpected expense after another has arisen—car repairs in large quantities, school financial requirements, dental bills, and so on. Thankfully my husband's company pays him for overtime hours, and no shortage of work exists at present. Unfortunately, those extra hours mean that he works every day till eight or nine o'clock at night. I am weary from holding down the fort alone.

Do I doubt that God loves me today? Emphatically no! However, I must confess that I do not feel His love today. A time like this requires several things from me, none of which I feel capable of at the moment. First, I need

---

[41] Strong's Concordance of the Bible #2638

faith or trust that what God says about His love for me remains true whether or not I feel it.

During a phone conversation with my husband a moment ago, I broke down in tears. I remain helpless to fix my circumstances or my emotions, so after saying goodbye, I fall to my knees and cry to the Lord. *Lord, strengthen me with power through your Spirit in my inner being that Christ might dwell in my heart through faith. Cause me to trust that what you say about loving me remains true even when my circumstances prove less than desirable, and when my heart feels sad. Amen.*

Now, I sit here contemplating the next thing for me to do in light of what the Love Prayer says about grasping the love of Christ. Like my dog eagerly pursues the tennis ball to grasp it for himself, I too must eagerly seek to possess Christ's love for myself. Feelings cannot deter me. God empowers this grasping, but He still uses my intellect. God wants me to comprehend with **my mind** the truth of His love for me. The evidence abounds, if I will but choose to allow my Savior to bring it to mind.

Do you ever get in a rut with your thoughts? You know, when all you can see is the negative? I know I do. So, this becomes my starting point for grasping the love of Christ--Get out of that rut! When asked, the Spirit will faithfully call to mind Scriptural truth of God's love for me, as well as the many tangible proofs of His loving work throughout my life. Through the Holy Spirit my focus shifts.

The act of knowing

However, it does not end there. Something remains missing, which brings us to the next action word in the Love Prayer--*know*. I have chosen to eagerly seek God's provision that I might grasp His love, but I also need to **_know_ this love that surpasses knowledge** as Paul says in verse nineteen. To grasp the love of Christ with my mind proves insufficient. For sure, it is a great starting point, but God wants me to also **know** His love with my heart. How is it possible to know something that goes beyond knowledge? Answer: I feel it!

Now, we all know that we must not base our faith on feelings. The obvious reality though is that God designed humans to feel love, not mentally analyze or merely store up facts about it in our gray matter. Support for this interpretation of the word *know* comes from its many Greek meanings. Several of those meanings relate to feelings and perceptions, not cold, hard facts. It should not be surprising then, that Paul's intended meaning in the phrase, *to know this love that surpasses knowledge*, is indeed an emotional one.

The apostle Paul wrote this inspired prayer for humans, so let us think of this in human terms: How does a person know that he or she is loved? Of course there must be evidence of that love. When it comes right down to it though, that evidence leads a person to sense, feel, and just *know* that they are loved.

When I fell in love

When I discussed this concept with my husband, he reminded me of his uncertainty when he and I first started spending time together in college. After a time of getting to know Seth, I realized that he was everything I had been praying for in a husband. Being insecure though, he did not recognize all of the signs indicating my feelings for him, and therefore; I had to patiently wait for him to ask me out. (Of course my roommate enjoyed teasing me in the interim.)

Our college had a cafeteria that was open for the dorm students to eat in three times a day. Like clockwork the students would form a line leading into the cafeteria at meal time, and I would just happen to find my way into the line at the same time Seth arrived. (Conveniently, my dorm room window provided the perfect view of the guys walking from their dorm to the cafeteria.) Then, of course, it was only natural to sit at the same table, in order to continue the conversation that had started in line. Often, we would sit in the cafeteria, talking long after the other students had left.

I remember desperately wanting to attend an upcoming homecoming banquet. Dreaming of an invitation from Seth, I turned down someone else's invitation. However, it never even occurred to Seth that I would want to go with him, so we both missed the event.

Another time, he was in the school cafeteria cleaning the ice-cream machine on a Friday night-- one of his college jobs. Meanwhile, I wandered the halls of the main building on campus in hopes of just happening to run into him. Coming across Sam, one of his friends, I casually inquired about Seth's whereabouts. Sam grinned slyly, like he knew why I really asked, and happily directed me into the cafeteria.

Only one good reason exists why a woman would use a Friday night to sit and watch a man work on a machine, and the ear-to-ear grin that was plastered on my face as we talked only served to indicate that reason. Although the evidence of my feelings for him should have been apparent, Seth still made no attempt to further the relationship-- even though he did seem pleased to have me with him while he worked.

Soon after that Friday night, Seth went with several of our friends to one of their homes for Thanksgiving break. Meanwhile, I went home to my family and impatiently counted down the days and hours until I would see him again. Upon arriving back on campus, I spotted him in the college cafeteria. My huge, silly grin embarrassingly appeared to greet him. After eating with our friends, we went out to his truck to listen to a music tape that I had brought him. Surely now he would recognize my sincere interest! No such luck. Although he was crazy about me, he still hedged his bets in spite of a mountain of evidence regarding my feelings for him.

We finally went on our first date before Christmas break. By the time we returned to school after break, the abundant evidence of my love finally caused him to decide that he *knew* I really did love him. He, in response, felt confident enough to declare his love for me. All doubt was gone, and a year later we married.

When the doubts go by the wayside, we feel loved and can respond in kind. This is true in human relationships like Seth's and mine, and it also proves true in our relationship with God. Once we truly *know* (feel) God's love, our response follows naturally.

Just as Seth was loved by me before grasping it (seizing it eagerly with the mind) and knowing it (feeling it with the heart), so also God loves you even if you do not grasp and know it. The existence of His love for you does not depend on your understanding or your feelings. However, until you know that love for yourself, you will not experience it as God intends.

I know the saying, *Love's not a feeling. It's an act of the will.* I agree, with reservations. Yes, feelings fluctuate back and forth based on all kinds of things--our hormones, the weather, how we slept the night before, etc. Certainly love does not depend on such irregularities. Any married individual of more than ten years knows that times come when the feelings diminish, but through an act of your will (otherwise known as commitment) you press on until the feelings return. However, if it takes a long time for those loving feelings to return, a tremendous struggle ensues. Commitment is noble and necessary, but oh, how agonizing the relationship becomes. That is because God designed His prize creations to feel, not just to analyze and interpret information.

Verse nineteen says that this love of God that we should be trying to eagerly possess (grasp) surpasses knowledge. In other words, you cannot know it with your mind! (Remember the last chapter that detailed the limitless nature of this love?) Therefore, knowing God's love is not just an act of your will, He means for it to be felt. Verses eighteen and nineteen of the Love Prayer prove that.

Last night, through tears I told my husband of my discouragement. He patiently listened and then communicated his love for me through words of understanding and encouragement. When we crawled into bed, he said, *Come here;* and we curled up together like a pair of spoons, while he caressed me. I fell asleep feeling loved and greatly encouraged knowing that I can face the world's demands with the love of my man.

A good husband does not want his wife to just take his love by faith but wants her to truly feel loved. Why? Because he knows that when she feels loved, she responds differently. Similarly, God has given you the gentle words of His unfailing love in the Bible, and you must eagerly grasp onto those words intellectually. However, the loving Savior desires more than that for you. He wants you to feel

His love as well. When you do, you will respond differently in your relationship with Him.

If you struggle with believing God loves you, as I did, then it can also be difficult to trust Him. It might possibly even prove difficult to love yourself and others. You might know, by faith in the truth of God's Word, that God loves you, but until you feel it, your response to God will always be a struggle.

Taking this into account, Paul insightfully requests that we will first eagerly seize God's love and then know (feel; perceive) it as well. Ask God for the final proof that we humans need in order to accept and act upon someone's love—a sense of certainty, yes; a wonderful, glorious feeling of being loved. Because God knows that we could never know with our minds a love so infinite that it surpasses knowledge, He wants us also to truly feel His love with our hearts.

I hope the thought of not just mentally acknowledging that God loves you, but also experiencing that love, excites you and gives you hope? Start praying. Your heavenly Father really does want to answer this life changing prayer for you!

Part 4

Trust

CHAPTER 11

Fill'er Up!

that you may be filled to the measure of all the fullness of God. (Ephesians 3:19b)

At different times through the years I have seen stores advertise a shopping spree as the grand prize for their particular sweepstakes. The thought of winning such a prize sparks the imagination. Who would not want to fill a cart to the rim at their favorite department store with as much merchandise as they desire! If such an opportunity were yours, would you begin with a cart cluttered with trash, your bulky jacket, and an oversized purse? No! A completely empty cart and visions of expensive wares would be your starting point. At the signal, you would race to fill the basket with the best quality products in the store. Up one aisle and down the next—looking for things you previously only dreamed of owning. Stopping before you had packed the cart to complete fullness would never enter your mind.

Such a scene proves a fitting illustration for the final request of the Love Prayer—*that you may be filled to the measure of all the fullness of God* (vs.19b). Upon first reading that phrase I thought, *I don't know what that means for sure, but I definitely want it!* Now after lengthy study, I do know what it means, and I certainly do want it in my life, and you will also. The question to begin with then is what is meant by *the fullness of God*? Two stories from the life of Jesus provide biblical illustrations to help answer this question.

Filling the 5,000 to Fullness

The first of these accounts occurs at a time of great mourning for Jesus. Deeply grieved over the beheading of John the Baptist, Jesus tried to escape the crowds by traveling by boat to a *solitary place* (Matthew 14:13). However, five thousand men and their families heard of his whereabouts and eagerly follow him on foot to a hillside by the Lake of Galilee. Out of compassion for the people, Jesus ignored his own needs and stayed to minister to the people.

After a tiring day of healing the sick and teaching the multitude, evening approached. The disciples pointed out to Jesus the fact that the people need to eat, live far away, and have no means of acquiring food. In fact, the only food available among the crowd was five loaves and two fish. While the disciples fretted over the impossibility of the situation, Jesus calmly instructed them to seat the crowd in groups. He then said a blessing and begins to break off pieces of the food, giving it to his disciples, who then dispersed it to the crowd. Miraculously, the food kept multiplying until all were served. **Matthew 14:20** says, ***And they did all eat, and were filled; and they took up of the fragments that remained twelve baskets full*** (KJV). In this instance, people are fed, not just minimally to stave off their hunger, but to complete fullness or satisfaction.

Filling Empty Wine Jugs

Another time, the Gospels tell of a wedding feast taking place in Cana of Galilee, where the nightmare of every host occurs: The amount of provisions for the guests proved insufficient. In this case, the wine ran out. The servants rush about in distress over what they should do. Jesus' mother, knowing her son's capabilities, informed him of the problem. In spite of his protests, Mary ordered the servants to carry out any action Jesus required of them.

Fill the jars with water, Jesus told the servants, and so they filled them to the brim (John. 2:7). In accordance with his exact instructions, they then drew out some of the liquid and took it to the master of the banquet. The master, unaware of the origin of the liquid, declared his astonishment that the bridegroom would save the best wine for the end of the feast when people's senses were already dulled by previous drinks. Apparently, wine made by the Master is astounding! This account showed how Jesus took empty jars and filled them to overflowing with satisfying wine. Still today Jesus continues to transform, through His own sufficiency, our meager offerings, and satisfies; not only partially, but fully.

Superabundant Fullness

Now, let us consider how the fullness or filling that Jesus accomplished in those two stories relates to the phrase in the Love Prayer, *that you may be filled to the measure of all the fullness of God* (vs.19b). The meaning of two similar words—filled and fullness—makes a good starting point. The two Bible stories just related use those two words just as the Love Prayer does. The root word for both words is the same and literally means *to cram (a net).*[42] Now can you see why I said that a shopping spree made a good analogy? Instead of a fishing net crammed full, we ladies can envision a cart crammed full!

Although definitions prove tedious, bear with me for a moment more that we might gain an accurate picture of the fullness of God. Very simply put, the word *fullness*

---

[42] Strong's Exhaustive Concordance of the Bible #4137

means *repletion or completion.*[43] Everyone knows the word completion, but repletion bears defining. Webster's Dictionary defines it simply as *superabundant fullness.* Let me apply these definitions to our prayer by paraphrasing the last request. It can be accurately and descriptively read—that you may be absolutely crammed to the brim with the completeness and superabundant fullness of God. Wow! Sounds good; does it not? Remember the illustration of the shopping spree? Anyone given such a prize would want to cram that cart to its maximum capacity with good things. If the shopping cart represents you, then the abundance of valuable merchandise that fills every nook and cranny of the cart represents the fullness of God. Desiring an abundant life for us, Paul prays that we will be lacking in nothing because God has filled every aspect of our being with the satisfying completeness of Himself.

The New Bible Commentary has the following to say about this verse:

> *The tense of the verb 'filled' suggests that this experience is not looked upon as something gradually acquired, but is thought of as some positive experience of the believer* (1023).

In other words, Paul does not pray for a gradual filling to superabundance, but an experience that leaves the believer complete because of God's completeness. The

---

[43] Strong's Exhaustive Concordance of the Bible #4138

filling of the Holy Spirit that comes at the moment of salvation comes to mind as such an experience. Remember though; Paul wrote this prayer for those who are already saved. Therefore, although other passages do refer to the indwelling of the Spirit, this is not one of them.

Satisfaction in the Fullness of God

A few other passages in the New Testament use the same Greek word for the fullness of God. For example, **Colossians 2:9-10** says, ***For in Christ all the fullness of the Deity lives in bodily form, and you have been given fullness in Christ.*** Did you catch that? Because fullness exists in God, as the verse states, Christ also contains that fullness. Then Christ offers that same fullness to completion to believers.

Living in an affluent society where people consider things the mark of worth, so many people try to fill their emptiness with possessions instead of God. I am not just speaking of unbelievers either. How many of us Christians remain continually discontent? Do we seem to live for the next big event, coveted possession, vacation or even relationship? Why do believers fall into that trap? The Love Prayer indicates that it stems from personal emptiness, to one degree or another, due to a lack of feeling God's love.

If you recognize this tendency in yourself, repent today and ask God to do what only He can do: satisfy. Just as the Son of God filled the multitude to complete satisfaction with their meager offerings, so also does He want to satisfy you with Himself. And, just as Jesus had the servants fill empty jars to the brim with nothing more than water and transformed them into jars filled to capacity with good quality wine, so also can He take your emptiness and fill you completely. Jesus alone brings completion and repletion (superabundance), and He wants to do it for you at your request.

Emptying Before Filling

It is worth noting that the jars at the wedding feast had to be empty before Jesus had them filled. Jesus did not make this wine in jars that were partially filled with something already. If He had, His perfect wine would have been diluted with inferior wine. Similarly, if you had a pitcher of near empty milk in the refrigerator that had turned rancid, would you pour fresh milk in with it? Certainly not! Instead, you would empty the pitcher completely before filling it anew or else the old milk would spoil the new.

Likewise, God may need to do some emptying in your life before He answers your prayer to fill you completely with His fullness. When I began to earnestly pray this part of the Love Prayer for myself, I did not expect the emptying that God would first do in me. Even though I had let go of my anger towards God regarding my son being taken away, I still had so much pent-up hurt from that ordeal. Those feelings were not sinful, but they were filling my heart and mind, which prevented God from filling me completely.

In order to answer my prayer, God first had to empty me of those hurts. A few days after I began praying for God's filling, a conversation triggered the pain from the past. Quickly I excused myself. In the privacy of my bedroom, I finally wept long and hard over the memories of each individual hurt and shame that I had endured, as well as for the vicarious suffering of watching my three year old son's agony during that time.

Even though the sobbing episode surely seemed unpleasant at the time, the permeating sense of God's loving presence made it an unforgettable time in my spiritual journey. I felt as though God lovingly rocked me in His arms, eyes full of tears-- just as a parent would do if their child were hurt deeply. Scripture actually portrays this mental picture of God in numerous places. In **Jeremiah 14:17**, God told the prophet Jeremiah to tell the Israelites how He felt about them: *Let my eyes overflow with tears night and day without ceasing; for my virgin daughter-- my people-- has suffered a grievous wound, a crushing blow.* God knew the wounds I had endured, and

He grieved with me as a loving Father. Likewise, He grieves for your wounds.

Because David always spoke his heart to the Lord, the Psalms quickly come to mind when I think of Scriptures that deal with emotions. In one of them David says, *Pour out your hearts to him, for God is our refuge* (**Psalm 62:8**). Even though long overdue for pouring out my burden of pain to the Lord, my lack of trust in God's true love and my anger over my hurts had left me unable to do so. Only after God opened my eyes to His tremendous love for me could I pour out my heart to Him and find the safe haven or refuge for which I longed.

I admit that the emptying proves difficult, but pouring out your pain in a safe, loving context brings freedom. Just as pouring out your troubles to a trusted and loving friend brings release and perspective, how much more wonderful when done to the One who knows you better than you know yourself and loves you immensely anyway? Perhaps like me you need this necessary step before the filling can occur.

Praise be to God that a knowledge of the love of Christ does not end the requests in the Love Prayer. Instead, God desires an even deeper experience for you: *that ye might be filled with all the fullness of God.*

You can offer the Savior your emptiness, dissatisfaction, and meager findings and let Him transform them into a completeness that fills every aspect of your person with Himself. Oh, the joy, peace, and contentment that will bring.

CHAPTER 12

Above & Beyond

*Now to him who is able to do immeasurably more
than all we ask or imagine, according to his power
that is at work within us, to him be glory in the
church and in Christ Jesus throughout all generations,
forever and ever! Amen."*

(Ephesians 3:20-21)

Have you ever had to ask multiple favors of
someone? Did you cringe at having to bother them for yet
another request? Only desperation could push you to be so
bold, and you would not have blamed them for saying no.
At some point, I suppose most everyone has had to do this.
My husband once told me of a co-worker of his who had
experienced the epitome of such a scenario. Upon hearing
the story, I asked my husband to write the amusing account
down so that I might include it as an illustration for this
book.[44] He graciously complied.

---

[44] I have included Seth Julin's writing in its entirety.

He writes, *One of my co-workers, whom I will call Joe, said that when he was a teenager, he and his brother had a job delivering newspapers to a rural area on the outskirts of Minneapolis. Though their route consisted mostly of farm houses and country homes, it was close enough to the growing metropolis that the government planning authorities deemed it necessary to install sewer and other utilities throughout the area.*

As a result of the digging necessary to install these lines, a number of the roads these brothers had to traverse in the darkness of pre-dawn morning were almost impassable. One road in particular, that they were required to navigate, had a portion so severely mangled that when they tried to pass through it at about four o'clock one morning, their wheels became hopelessly mired in the soupy clay that is common in that part of the country.

As they struggled with their problem, it became apparent rather quickly that no amount of pushing, digging or changing gears would get them out of the mud hole in which they found themselves, and they were forced to admit that they needed help. But, help was not easy to find in that area at that hour. This was long before the advent of cell-phones. There were also no pay phones or all-night businesses within walking distance, and no headlights or noises forecasted the approach of another vehicle.

It was only them, their stuck car, the night sounds...and one very dark farm house nearby; its occupants sound asleep. After some discussion they decided that the only viable option at their disposal was to rouse the inhabitants of the farm house and hope that the response would be one of the more pleasant scenarios that could result. So, with much trepidation these brothers resigned themselves to knocking on a stranger's door.

It was a surprised and confused man of the house who finally unbolted the door and peered out at the two hapless young men. They communicated their situation to him and asked if he would be willing to allow them the use of his telephone, so that help could be summoned.

Under the circumstances a grumpy reply and a slammed door might have been about the response Joe could have expected. But, to his surprise, the man not only agreed to allow them use of the telephone but also suggested that they first allow him to see if he could help them get their vehicle out.

He walked out to the road with the brothers, and with the extra muscle, plus the ingenuity and wisdom of an older man, they were successful in getting their car out of the mud. The residents of that area awoke later and retrieved their newspapers, never knowing the effort that had been expended to make this possible.

This would be the end of the story, except for one thing: Joe and his brother still had their newspaper route, and in order to perform the duties related to that route, they had no choice but to continue using that road. So it was that on two other occasions the brothers were forced to knock on the door of this same house, each time before five in the morning. And on each occasion, they were greeted, not by a slamming door, an angry shout or a shotgun full of rock-salt, but by a man who gave them what they requested and offered to do even more.

In small scale, this real-life example illustrates what we find in the Love Prayer. Imagine the difficulty for Joe and his brother to knock on that stranger's door once, let alone to do so again and again. The stranger would have been justified in ignoring the four a.m. knocks at his door, but instead, he went beyond what they asked or hoped by offering to personally fix the problem.

The three requests of the Love Prayer

The Love Prayer's major requests, as detailed in the previous chapters, amount to colossal interventions on God's part. Because each request deals with critical issues, if resolved they would have phenomenal implications for our relationship with God, causing an outpouring of positive changes in our daily lives. Let us take a moment to remember the requests from the prayer:

- To begin, we pray that God will strengthen us with power in our inner being. This empowerment would serve to make it possible to trust Christ, allowing Him to dwell in a hospitable environment (a heart of trust).

- Secondly, we request that we would be able to grasp (eagerly seize) Christ's love for us in order that we might know (feel and experience) its magnitude.
- In keeping with the significance of the other requests, the prayer lastly beseeches the Lord to wholly fill us with the completeness that only God can bring, leaving us lacking nothing.

Whew! Christian counselors dream of success in helping their clients to achieve just one of those, say nothing of all three!

A *quadriplegic's desire*

While not wanting to sound overly dramatic, the life altering impact of those spiritual requests can be compared in significance to a quadriplegic praying for the complete healing of all his limbs. Bear with me a moment while we consider the analogy. What if a quadriplegic began praying for healing? Thinking complete use of all his limbs too much to pray for, what if he instead asked only for a working right arm? Yes, a working arm would give him many more capabilities, just as a person's ability to trust God would positively affect several areas of his or her life. But, partial physical healing proves no match for the complete life transformation that would occur in a quadriplegic if he regained the full use of both arms and legs. Physically he would be whole again. Similarly, the resolution of all three heart issues of the Love Prayer would make the recipient of these gifts spiritually and emotionally whole.

As I initially prayed this prayer, I found myself thinking it was too much to ask and certainly too much to truly expect God to do in my life. That attitude compares well with, *Just one working arm would be good enough, Lord.* If God had intended, however, to stop with just one of these answered requests, He would not have inspired Paul to write all of them in one prayer. God has always desired to do more than all I can ask or imagine, which leads us to the meaning of the next verse of the prayer.

An overabundance of superlatives

Most fittingly, the Love Prayer concludes with a doxology. Paul, very aware of the significance of the requests, desires to bring attention to God's limitless power to accomplish them. In fact, the verse overflows with superlatives emphasizing God's capability. In the King James Version, the first half of the verse reads, *Now unto him that is able to do exceeding abundantly above all that we ask or think* (vs.20a). The New International Version says, *Now to him who is able to do immeasurably more than all we ask or imagine* (vs.20a).

My loose paraphrase of Paul's words goes like this: **You know all of those major, life-changing requests I**

just prayed? **Not only can God answer those, but He can do even more than you ever imagined and in a more amazing way than you ever dreamed possible.** No fallback plan exists if this does not work out. God can do it; period.

The third mention of power

Although the first statement of verse 20 staggers the mind, the truly intriguing part follows and ends the verse. How can God can do way beyond what you could even think to ask? The answer: *According to his power that is at work within us* (vs.20b). When I took notice of that phrase for the first time, awe overcame me. Because the Holy Spirit's miraculous power (*dunamis*) indwells me, God can do anything in me and through me. That power is available for use in gaining the greatly desired and much needed changes prayed for in Ephesians 3.

2 Peter 1:3 further explains this concept when it says that God, *According as his divine power hath given unto us all things that pertain unto life and godliness, through the knowledge of him that hath called us to glory and virtue* (KJV). What an incredible concept: God has given us everything we need to live abundant, godly lives.

Our backgrounds, ineptitude, hang-ups and various other shortcomings show us to be inadequate without God. Mathematically speaking, we just do not add up to sufficient people. But, when God becomes the missing variable, His children become far more than adequate. Try and wrap your mind around the biblically stated fact that God has already placed in the believer the power necessary to far exceed their greatest expectations? Truly mind boggling!

From fearful farmer to mighty warrior

This calls to my mind the Old Testament story of Gideon. In the book of Judges we learn about a simple farmer living at a time when the Israelites had abandoned God. Consequently, God allowed His people to undergo severe oppression by the Midianites. The Israelites finally cried out to God for help, and so the Lord chose an unlikely character to bring deliverance for them.

Even though the angel of the Lord found Gideon threshing his wheat in hiding for fear of the Midianites, the angel addressed him by saying, *The LORD is with you, mighty warrior* **(Judges. 6:12)**. The angel then goes on to say, *Go in the strength you have and save Israel out of Midian's hand* **(vs.14)**. Gideon's shock came out in his reply, *But Lord...how can I save Israel? My clan is the weakest in Manasseh, and I am the least in my family"* **(vs.15)**.

I can relate to that. Have you ever been asked to do something in ministry or just felt God's prompting of you to do something for Him? Did you quickly list out a number of reasons that God should find someone far more suited to the task than you? Not surprisingly, the response of inadequacy also dictated Gideon's response and apparently for good reason.

Why then, does the angel refer to Gideon as a mighty warrior when he obviously was not? Perspective. Gideon saw only his current shortcomings. God, however, saw all that God's power in him would accomplish. Did you notice how the angel's greeting began with, *The LORD is with you.*? God's presence brings with it tremendous power! After much encouragement and a couple, reassuring signs from the Lord, Gideon lead the tiny Israelite army (culled by God to be small) to victory over the vast Midianite army. Choosing the weak to shame the proud, God's power worked in and through a humble farmer. As a result, a mighty warrior and a free Israelite nation were formed.

Power to bring God glory

This same power, which did the miraculous in and through Gideon's life, works now in every believer. God is just waiting to put it to use! The first verse of the doxology reassures us that God can handle the three huge requests in the Love Prayer. Furthermore, God waits expectantly to use His power within us to transform us more than we can ask or imagine.

Because the odds were completely against the success of Gideon and the Israelite army, God alone received the glory when they triumphed. Similarly, the power working in us should also render glory to the source of that power—God. This leads us to the next verse of the prayer's doxology, which reads, *To him be glory in the church and in Christ Jesus..."* (**vs.21**).

Where this glory comes from holds significance. Though several New Testament verses speak of individual believers bringing God glory, this verse specifies that God should receive glory from *the church and in Christ Jesus* (**vs.21**). Why does Paul make this distinction at the end of a very personal prayer for people as individuals?

A reminder of God's tool

Do you remember earlier in the book the phrase that I discussed; *may have power, together with all the saints* (Ephesians 3:18a)? In that phrase, Paul connects the power of Christ in us with the corporate body. He does it again in this doxology when he says, *according to the power that is at work within us, to him be the glory in the church and in Christ Jesus* (vs. 20-21).

Those two phrases, however, do not stand alone as the only indicators that Paul wants to end the prayer with the focus on how God's power in us should tie us to His Body, the church. It is significant to note that Paul also switches from the consistent and sole use of the personal pronoun *you* in the first four verses of the prayer, to the plural pronouns *us* and *we* in the doxology. Why is that? By shifting the prayer from personal and individual to corporate, the apostle aims for a conclusion that reminds us of the big picture-- that God's power doing amazing things in individuals serves to benefit the church, thereby bringing God glory. The individuals do the work of the church, which serves as God's means or tool for bringing Himself glory on this earth.

Does the tool or the operator get the praise?

Let me give an illustration. Have you ever tried to dig a hole without a shovel, cut a board without a saw, or make a cake without a mixer? The proper tool can be worth its weight in gold when needed.

However, once you accomplish the task, who gets the credit for a job well done--the tool or the operator? When you finish building your deck and then have a bar-b-que with friends, who gets the compliments? Would your friends say, *You must have one terrific table saw to be able to make this deck!*? Or, how about when you serve a delicious chocolate cake you made and everyone wishes their waistline would allow for more? Is it likely that you would hear them say, *Your mixer did an incredible job mixing up such a tasty cake!*? Why not? After all, the tools did cut the boards and mix the batter. Yes, but without your ingenuity and physical power the tools prove worthless.

I often think of myself as merely a tool in the Master's hands when I do anything for God. I may technically do the work, but without God's power working through me, I am just a helpless tool. Likewise, the church also serves as a tool in the Master's hands, being used to work His good purposes on this earth.

You may recall that in chapter four, I discuss Paul's teaching on the body of Christ, and that Jesus exists as the head of that body. In this doxology *the two... are looked upon as inseparable,* according to The New Bible Commentary (1023). That commentary goes on to say that **Ephesians 1:22-23** clearly identifies this relationship by stating,

> **And God placed all things under his feet and appointed him to be head over everything for the church, which is his body, the fullness of him who fills everything in every way.**

On this earth, glory comes to God when His tool, the Body of Christ, has fullness in Him. God's perfect plan allows for individuals to function within the Body, under the headship of Christ. When Christians do this, the Body works as a whole unit, with each part doing its work in harmony with the other members and all for the glory of God.

Benefiting the Body of Christ

God does not desire for lone Christians to try to remain as separate entities. Let me use myself as an example. By radically changing my spiritual perspective, God has brought about positive changes in my life such as freedom from tremendous burdens of pain, guilt, anger, mistrust of God, and feelings of being unloved and unaccepted by Him. Yet, so many others still struggle under those vexatious burdens. Do you think for a second that God brought about such an amazing work in my life for my benefit alone? No. Loving others just as much as He loves me, God wants all to know the same freedom and joy that I now know. Without a doubt, it would be wrong of me to do my own thing, apart from the church, selfishly hoarding the gifts God has given me.

God even states such in **2 Corinthians 1:3-4**.

Praise be to the God and Father of our Lord Jesus Christ, the Father of compassion and the God of all comfort, who comforts us in all our troubles, so that we can comfort those in any trouble with the comfort we ourselves have received from God.

God clearly wants me to share with others what He has done for me, so that His body can benefit. **Luke 12:48** says, *From everyone who has been given much, much will be demanded; and from the one who has been entrusted with much, much more will be asked.* These verses make it evident that I must not hoard God's blessings to myself by being isolated from His Body, nor should any other believer.

Perhaps you agree but believe that you cannot possibly benefit anyone in the church right now because of unresolved issues. Perhaps you currently find yourself incapable of giving much to the Body due to physical issues. Possibly this is a season for you to personally experience the benefit of God's tool of love in your life.

Quite possibly though, God wants to use you, just as He did with Gideon, in spite of weakness in order to bring glory to Himself,. Therefore, prayerfully consider what God would have you do or not do at this stage of your life. In the Body of Christ, whether you minister to others or the Body ministers to you, God gets the glory.

To all the courses of the age of the ages

In the last words of the prayer, Paul uses the strongest wording possible to make it understood that God will be glorified for all time. He says, *Throughout all generations, forever and ever. Amen* (**vs.21b**) The

Wycliffe Bible Commentary puts it this way: *God's glory is being manifested throughout all eternity in the body which he has redeemed.* When translated, the phrase for eternity used in verse twenty-one literally means, *to all the courses of the age of the ages* (738). The last word of the prayer is *Amen*, meaning, *so be it.* It does not get more final than that!

And so the prayer ends with the emphatic statement that God has given us miraculous power capable of bringing about the life-changing requests made previously. The Almighty One provides the power so that He receives glory through His church. As a result, He accomplishes incredible miracles in the lives of people, in spite of, and in fact, because of, their weaknesses.

Therefore, persist in praying this prayer with great confidence to the God *who is able to do immeasurably more than all we ask or imagine, according to his power that is at work within us*, and watch in amazement at the transformation.

CHAPTER 13

An End of Fear

There is no fear in love. But perfect love drives out fear,
because fear has to do with punishment. The man who
fears is not made perfect in love. (I John 4:18)

A friend of mine once asked me an interesting
question in the form of an illustration. He said that he
pictures our access to God through prayer as if we all wait
in a long line to present our requests to the God of the
Universe. Of course, those who are more righteous stand at
the front of the line. He wanted to know why I, being in his
estimation, far more righteous than he, did not get bumped
to the front of the line for immediate relief of my suffering?

Now, I know that nothing in the Bible corroborates
such a view of our access to God. Instead, we can each
gain access to God's throne room simultaneously through
the righteousness of Christ. However, my friend's question
does illustrate an interesting human perspective on how
many think God prioritizes the prayers of His saints.

Surely, the incredibly devoted and righteous apostle Paul would have had a pass to the front of the line at all times. Why, therefore, would he not gain an earthly cessation to his sufferings? And, since he did not, how could he possibly continue to trust God's love for him personally? Instead of doubt, he trusted God with such an astounding depth that he viewed his many sufferings in a whole different light. Although I discussed these questions at the start of this book, I wish to revisit our starting point in order to draw conclusions.

Suffering seen through a different lens

Upon my reflection of Paul's astounding perspective, a recent event came to mind. A young girl from my church, whom I will call Sarah, underwent surgery for an abdominal problem. Having weeks to anticipate the surgery, this ten year old girl worked herself up into quite a terrified frenzy at the prospect. Not surprisingly, her mother asked the church to pray for her daughter.

After the surgery was over and Sarah had recovered, I asked her mother about the experience. She replied that the pain proved far worse than Sarah or her parents had anticipated the first day after surgery, but that it then decreased steadily over the next several days. As you might expect, I expressed my sympathy for her daughter's suffering. *Oh, Sarah would gladly go through it again*, she surprisingly responded with a chuckle. *You see*, she elaborated, *Sarah was queen of the house during her recovery. She reclined on the couch while we all waited on her hand-and-foot and took turns entertaining her. We purchased every age-appropriate game sold and played them with our daughter. I also arranged for all of Sarah's friends to come separately to spend time with her until she fully recovered.*

Consequently, Sarah looked at her painful ordeal through a different lens. The surgery and recovery did not hurt any less, but her parents demonstrated their love for her in a way unlike any other time in her life. The parental love for their daughter, and the blessings that love brought, so completely transformed Sarah's perspective on the pain she suffered that she would even willingly go through it again. Wow!

Let us consider how the story of Sarah sheds light on Paul's perspective in the words leading up to the Love Prayer. The apostle spoke of one of the rich blessings as God's children-- direct access to God. Surprisingly, he goes immediately from talking about that blessing to mentioning his sufferings. Consider for a moment those seemingly contradictory concepts: Direct access to God-- suffering not ended. Why would Paul not have grown discouraged? The answer lies in the illustration of Sarah's ordeal.

If Sarah were asked to give evidence for how she knows that her parents love her deeply, would she not point to a time when she endured great pain yet received an outpouring of parental care? The love she already knew, now stood out with greater intensity on a backdrop of suffering. I too, can look back at times of suffering and see God's work in a myriad of ways on my behalf. No, He did not take away the painful circumstances of living in a fallen world, but He did show Himself loving in countless ways.

Paul knew this to be true when he penned the introduction to the Love Prayer. Once the apostle grasped and knew the depth of God's love, as well as God's eternal purpose for man, he viewed his sufferings as only a list of momentary problems. No doubt existed in his mind that God in His goodness would use Paul's suffering for good. That view of God's incredible love produced complete trust.

My journey to change

Although God gave me a mental understanding of these matters early on in the writing of this book, I did not grasp and experience it personally until recently. Most authors write as experts on their chosen topic before they ever set ink to paper. Such was not the case with this book. When I first began writing, I did so with more questions than answers, more pain than joy, more anger than forgiveness, and more personal condemnation than acceptance. I have shared my spiritual journey with you in the pages of this book as it has transpired, and what an incredible journey these months have been. I knew when I first began contemplating the words of the Love Prayer that it must contain the answers I sought, but I never could have dreamed of the transformation that God would bring about in answer to my praying this prayer.

Nothing has changed in these months regarding my past or current physical suffering except for my perspective on them. It might be easy for me to tell you that I now feel loved by God and trust Him if my health problems had ended. Although they have improved; by no means have they ended. As I type these words, my abdomen churns and hurts, my back still announces its existence with sharp reminders, and I know that I can not possibly do the physically active things that I dream of doing. However, I actually find myself excited about living for the first time in years. I walk around the house singing praises to my Savior and Lord. Why? Because I am now on antidepressants –No! It is because I am completely, unfailingly, and unconditionally loved and accepted by my God, and because of that I do not have to live in fear of the future anymore.[45]

---

[45] After the completion of this book, I updated, revised, and edited it for six years during which time God has done an incredible work in me physically. Go to http://www.heartandmindministries.com/#!heartpeace/c23kk to hear the story--A Heart at Peace.

Have you ever had one of those *A hah!* moments when things suddenly make sense? Such a moment came for me recently when I read **1 John 4:18**. Without mincing words, it says, ***There is no fear in love. But perfect love drives out fear, because fear has to do with punishment. The one who fears is not made perfect in love.*** These words show the direct connection between not knowing God's love and the resulting, inappropriate fear of God. That verse summarizes why I used to dread the future. How could I possibly trust God with my life or my future while being convinced that He did not love me personally? I could not! However, once the Lord convinced me of His abiding love, the fear came to an end and joy filled my heart--***perfect love drives out fear.***

A spirit of fear

At what level would you rate your fear and anxiety? Do you join the growing ranks of individuals who suffer with anxiety? Perhaps you would instead characterize your thoughts in this area with more mild terms such as *apprehensive, concerned, or stressed.* As I speak with other women, I hear frequent discussions on panic attacks, medications being used to combat anxiety, or just obsessive fretting and worrying over everything from the weather to their children's activities. For some, worst case scenarios plague their minds on a daily basis. It seems so normal and appropriate. Fear and anxiousness seem to be Christianity's acceptable--do I dare say it--sin.

How dare I suggest such a thing, you might think. However, **Romans 14:23** says, *everything that does not come from faith is sin.* The Father tells us in His Word not to fear over three hundred and sixty-five times. Why? If God is a god of peace, then fear and anxiousness remain contrary to His Spirit that lives in us. This would be why **Romans 8:14-16** says,

> *For those who are led by the Spirit of God are the children of God. The Spirit you received does not make you slaves, so that you live in fear again; rather, the Spirit you received brought about your adoption to sonship. And by him we cry, "Abba, Father." The Spirit himself testifies with our spirit that we are God's children.*

Let me summarize those verses. If you are truly a child of God, then you no longer have to be controlled by a spirit of fear. According to Romans 6, the old nature died with Christ so that we no longer have to be slaves to this fear that once ruled us. We have a new nature--a spirit of sonship that allows us to cry, *Daddy* to the LORD God Almighty.

Do you remember the illustration I gave at the beginning of the book from the movie, The King and I? That little girl could race unceremoniously into the throne room and jump right into her Daddy, the king's arms to receive help. What a beautiful picture of perfect love casting out fear! And why, because her daddy loves her, is powerful, and therefore; she can trust him to work good on her behalf.

God longs for His children to trust Him fully. Fear in itself is just a human emotion like anger. To have fear cannot be a sin for Jesus certainly experienced a host of negative emotions, including fear as he contemplated the suffering to come at the cross. In **John 12:27** Jesus says, *Now my heart is troubled, and what shall I say? "Father, save me from this hour?" No, it was for this very reason I came to this hour. "Father, glorify your name!"* In other words, feeling troubled, anxious, despair, and fear do not make one a sinner. But just as in the case of anger, what you do in response to those emotions can be the problem. Jesus felt the fear, but knew His Father's perfect will could be trusted regardless. As a result, Jesus continued His work, did nothing to avoid situations that inevitably would bring Him suffering, and walked in peace.

When God revealed His perfect plan to Moses for delivering God's people from Egyptian slavery, Moses balked in fear. The loving Father understood Moses' human frailty, and so God responded with encouragement and signs of power. Eventually, though, there came a time when it became apparent that Moses intended to cling to his fears rather than trust in his Almighty God, and *then the LORD's anger burned against Moses.*[46] Moses crossed the line from understandable emotion to disobedience because of that emotion.

---

[46] Exodus 3:7-4:14

God longs for His children to trust in Him. He understands our weaknesses, and has given us all that we need to walk in obedience according to a spirit of sonship, not fear. When we choose to walk according to the flesh and obsess rather than trust, we sin and must repent. My hope for this discussion on fear is not to bring guilt or condemnation but to shed light on an area that Christians often ignore.

Perhaps you have read the preceding paragraphs and think that I am suggesting you buck up and start trying harder to conquer fear's control over you. Nothing could be farther from the truth. What does Scripture say casts out fear?--self effort, determination, perseverance...? No. *Perfect love casts out fear. The one who fears is not made perfect in love.* Grasping and knowing the love of Christ in its limitlessness provides the antidote to fear.

I too have wrestled greatly for a lifetime with fear's consuming power. However, thanks to the precious words of the Love Prayer and God's faithfulness to answer those requests for me, I can now rest in His love. The fear has been driven out! It truly is the most amazing change! **He has *strengthened* me *with power, through his Spirit, in* my *inner being so that Christ might dwell in* my *heart through faith* (Ephesians 3:16).** Praise be to God! Hopefully with God's continued strengthening, I will handle the trials of this life, that are certain to come, with confidence in God's love and plan for me instead of with fear. I now know with certainty that God, because He loves me as His child, truly will work together for my good, all things. That does not mean the suffering will hurt any less, but like little Sarah, the correct perspective of that pain brings joy and not despair. Only God could do such a work in one such as me. Praise be to God—my Maker, Redeemer and friend!

Let me ask you to consider the following question: Are you able to rest in God, truly trusting Him to get you through a particular trial, or do you find yourself continually afraid, stressed, or worried about life's hurdles? Ultimately, this boils down to whether or not you question His love for you. Remember, *perfect love drives out fear.*

He can do it in you!

You too can be convinced in your spirit of Christ's personal, unfailing love for you no matter the circumstances. Paul certainly was, and I now am as well. I pray that you too will be. In order for the troubles of this life to not make us bitter, hurting Christians, we each need to fully experience God's love for us. We cannot possibly accomplish this on our own, and so Paul penned an eloquent prayer that takes our deepest need to Immanuel, God with us.

While I have hoped and prayed that the thoughts and words of this book would speak to your heart, illuminating the path before you, my words will fall short of changing such deep-rooted human struggles. Only God has the power capable of opening your eyes to His truth, and He makes it available to you for the asking. Therefore, I plead with you to continue praying and meditating on this prayer. Once you see the depth of God's love for you and His eternal purpose for your life, the painful times in life will become only momentary problems that God, in His goodness, will use for your good. May you one day join the psalmist David in saying, *I will praise you, O Lord, among the nations; I will sing of you among the peoples. For great is your love, higher than the heavens; your faithfulness reaches to the skies* (Psalm 108:3-4). The LORD's blessing be upon you.

The Love Prayer

(personalized)

I pray that out of his glorious riches he may strengthen me with power through his Spirit in my inner being, so that Christ may dwell in my heart through faith.

And I pray that I, being rooted and established in love, may have power, together with all the saints, to grasp how wide and long and high and deep is the love of Christ, and to know this love that surpasses knowledge— that I may be filled to the measure of all the fullness of God.

Now to him who is able to do immeasurably more than all I ask or imagine, according to his power that is at work within me, to him be glory in the church and in Christ Jesus throughout all generations, forever and ever! Amen.

Ephesians 3:16-21

Works Cited

Professor F. Davidson M.A., D. (Ed.). (1965). *The New Bible Commentary* (2nd ed.). Grand Rapids, Michigan: WM. B. Eerdmans Publishing Company.

The New Testament and Wycliffe Bible Commentary (3rd ed.). (1971). New York, New York: The Iversen Associates.

James Strong, S. L. *The Exhaustive Concordance of the Bible.* Peabody, Massachusetts: Hendrickson Publishers.

http://en.wikipedia.org/wiki/Yellowstone_National _Park#cite_note-geothermal-8

Scribner's Monthly Vol.III. November, 1871. No.1, "Thirty-seven Days of Peril." Everts, Truman C.

May I ask you a question? Moyer, Dr. Lary. Evan Tell.

"Tis So Sweet to Trust in Jesus." Kirkpatrick, William J. and Stead, Louisa M.R.

Reviews are treasured and appreciated by an author. If you enjoyed this book or even better still, found it helpful, would you please take a few minutes to offer your thoughts in a review on Amazon? Go to:

http://www.amazon.com

and search for "When You Can't Trust His Heart." On the book page will be an option for writing a review.

Thanks!

About the Author

Born in southern California but primarily raised in the Atlanta area, Marci Julin is one of four children. At a young age she heard the Gospel in a Baptist Sunday school class and responded by placing her trust in Jesus Christ for salvation. At 8 years old she felt the call of God to reach the lost with the Good News of Jesus Christ and had the unique privilege of spending her teenage summers on the mission field. That desire to see people come to saving faith in Jesus Christ never abated, but the realities of life prevented full-time service until she became an empty-nester.

While attending Bryan College, a Christian liberal arts college in Dayton, Tennessee, she met and married Seth, her husband now of 23 years. Before the birth of their son, they moved to the Orlando, Florida area to be near family and have continued to reside there. Although she graduated from Bryan with a bachelor's degree in elementary education and a minor in Bible, Marci chose to be a homemaker and home-school their only child, Caleb, through the 7th grade. She then taught for two years at her son's classical Christian school.

In spite of always feeling God's hand on her life and desiring to please Him, Marci struggled with depression and trusting that God loved her personally due to many years of plaguing health problems. As a type A, driven person she continued pushing herself to her physical limits, always striving to be perfect in everything in order to win the approval of her Lord. It wasn't until God allowed her to become bedridden that she was forced to deal with her misconceptions about God and His deep, unfailing love for her. As the merciful Savior brought healing to her heart and mind through Scripture, He also brought complete physical healing. She now wholeheartedly agrees with the Psalmist when he says, *It was good for me to be afflicted so that I might learn your decrees. The law from your mouth is more precious to me than thousands of pieces of silver and gold* (Psalm 119:71-72).

Since her son, Caleb left home in pursuit of a bachelor's degree at Bryan College, Marci began Heart & Mind Ministries and has devoted her time to biblical teaching, writing, and speaking. She also enjoys traveling and exploring the beautiful areas of God's amazing creation with her family, running, gardening, and studying God's Word. Although acutely aware of the sanctifying work that God still needs to accomplish in her, Marci longs to inspire others with a passion for God's Word and a love for her Savior.

- **Check her out on Facebook at https://www.prod.facebook.com/marci.julin.**
- **You can also follow her writing on her blog, *Full of Heart and Deep in Thought* https://www.heartandmindministries.com**

About Heart & Mind Ministries

Heart ✝ Mind Ministries
Colossians 2:2-3

Heart and Mind Ministries was born out of a desire by Marci Julin to inspire other Christian women to love God and His Word with passion and to seek to know Him more. Christians don't have to check their brains at the door to believe the Bible. We have a faith that stands up to the test of time, to the criticism of skeptics, and to personal scrutiny. We can and should ask difficult questions and dig deeply to study and understand the Scriptures. In addition, as women, God has created us to feel things deeply with our hearts. The women who were last at the cross and first at the tomb were motivated, not just by a knowledge of Jesus, but by an overwhelming love for Him.

God gifts each of His servants in unique ways, and Marci Julin's teaching embodies both a truly personal, and yet an intellectual approach. With a mind that seeks order and understanding Marci loves to dig deep for the treasures that abound in Scripture. Come join Marci in the pursuit by subscribing to her website, so that you do not miss any of the free resources she offers.

https://www.heartandmindministries.com

- **Schedule her to speak at your next women's event.** Contact her through the ministry's website.

47228604R00117

Made in the USA
Charleston, SC
06 October 2015